Connie Broome

BOOK

MW00938217

"This manual is much more than solid Biblical teaching on healing the sick. It is a manual that equips every believer how to walk in their God-given authority to command healing in Jesus name. This manual will encourage you to step out in faith and do what Jesus did: that is, to use healing, deliverance and miracles as a way to confirm the preaching of the Gospel to unbelievers. Also to demonstrate the love and power of God to those in need of a divine touch. For those who take this message to heart and put it into practice, they will see miraculous healings in their own lives and ministry. To God be the glory!"

~ Michael Peters, M.D.
Director-IHOPE Missions Base
Waterloo, Iowa, USA

■ ■ ■

"This manual is dynamic and has cutting edge revelation to equip the Body of Christ worldwide.

This is a must for all those who are seriously inclined on fulfilling their end time prophetic destiny in the Lord. It

Thank you for the impact you have head on my life.

Blessing ! Prophet Roshan Rambally 04/01/18

will cause a paradigm shift in your thinking and break the tradition as you step out and step into the 'how' to get it done as outlined in the manual.

I would encourage every 5-fold minister and believer in the Body of Christ to get a copy of this invaluable resource tool for divine equipping for action in the spirit as Jesus moves you by His Spirit into the realm of the miraculous."

~ Pastor Stanley Velaidam, Senior pastor
Peniel Outreach Ministry, Nigg, Berbice,
Guyana, South America

■ ■ ■

"I have personally known Prophet Rohan Rambally for many years now. I believe God's highest plans for His ministers, is to make the man of God first, in His image. I believe that Prophet Rohan Rambally is such a man.

Dr. Rohan Rambally is a man who follows after God - with his whole heart, and literally puts his all into his pursuit of God. It is a rare find to have a man who loves God, with all he has. A man who moves in the gifting's of God, and who walks it out in love. He is a true gift to the Body of Christ.

I have been in some of his meetings where I have literally seen the presence of the Holy Spirit who brings healing, signs, wonders. Dr. Rohan Rambally allows the Holy Spirit the freedom to move as He pleases, to set His people free.

Prophet Rohan Rambally, has put God's heart, and healing touch in a manual that will activate all who participate in what God has. I believe it is a time like no other and God is pouring out his Spirit in ways like never before. God has birthed within Prophet Rohan Rambally, his plan to release to the world through this manual and the gifting's.

Prophet Rohan Rambally, has a depth in the word of God it is evident in his writing and the ability to release it on paper and in teachings. He has laid a Scriptural basis and foundation for all who want to walk in the very footsteps of our master Jesus Christ. Signs, wonders and miracles follow them that believe. DO YOU BELIEVE? The manual will change your life. A MUST READ!"

~ Prophetess Kim Kurnow
Miracles of the Heart Ministries
Treasures of Heaven Ministries
Christian International Associate Minister
Florida and Hawaii

■ ■ ■

"There is a need for all believers but especially new believers to read this manual. It gives you a solid foundation on how healing works. The manual gives every scriptural situation on how Jesus did healing and how we are supposed to do things the same way He did. This manual lets you know when to minister healing and when to use your authority to see healing manifest. The manual has been written in a way that all will be able to understand the scriptural process to see healings established. It will be a blessing to all who read it and put into practice what is taught in this manual."

~ Tom Wass
Hamilton, Ontario
Canada

■ ■ ■

"We see this manual as an excellent reading/teaching/ studying material. It's written in a systematic order, well-researched and referenced with the use of scriptures to interpret scriptures. You will understand, as we have, how to effectively operate in your kingly office and the time and place for the other offices. Also, as we delved further into the chapters our curious minds were satisfied and misconceptions abated. It has challenged us to step out of the natural and into the supernatural with the authority and faith of God by 'Moving In The Miraculous'."

~ Pastors Richard & Denique Alexander of Wonderful Counsellor Ministries

Trinidad and Tobago
West Indies

■ ■ ■

"There is an obvious pressing need in the world today – people need to be healed of their sicknesses and diseases. Jesus said in Matthew 10:8 - Heal the sick, cleanse the lepers, raise the dead, cast out devils: freely ye have received, freely give. This manual would certainly equip believers to exercise their authority over personal sicknesses which is a great need amongst Christians and also empower them to apply the principles in faith to heal others and thereby assist in winning the lost for Christ. Let us all receive these Practical and Biblical instructions and follow our Saviour and Healer – Commanding Healing in the Name of Jesus."

~ Rev Rajkumar Meighoo
Senior Pastor of Central Missions Foundation
International Word of Life Centre – Talparo
Trinidad, West Indies

■ ■ ■

"No better person to write on the topic of divine healing, but Prophet Rohan Rambally. Here is a servant of the Lord who has a deep compassion for people and to see them be healed from every manner of sickness. This manual is a must-read for every believer. You can receive your healing even as you read this manual because of the power and authority with which it was written."

~ Evangelist Ruth Ramsingh
Deliverance Temple International Organisation,
30 Besson Street, Port of Spain Trinidad, West Indies

■ ■ ■

"This manual is easy to read and apply. The author does not go into any fanciful treatment of the subject on healing. No long drawn out stories, but one that we can put into practice immediately, and see if the content measures up with reality. We are asked to heal the sick, after reading this manual your faith would be increased to go and do what it says, that is, 'heal the sick'.

Indeed as was stated...It is very important that believers are first taught, trained, equipped and mentored in the kingly office in order to function in dominion and power. No fear, no doubt, just absolute faith."

~ Tyrone Dass, PhD (student) Mathematics at the University of the West Indies
MSc (Mathematics), at the University of the West Indies
BSc. (Mathematics) with honours at the University of London
Ag. Teacher III Mathematics at Couva West Secondary, Trinidad and Tobago, West Indies

■ ■ ■

"The same spiritual DNA that Jesus carried has been transferred to His saints. This DNA is what connects us spiritually to the anointing of God. It assists believers in understanding that we have a destiny that is grounded upon our relationship as sons and daughters in Him. Dr. Rohan Rambally takes this message to another level. Not only does his work bring revelation to the Body of Christ but it does so in a DNA anointing that is hard to deny. Expertly written and divinely researched the truths from this book are yours to keep. I highly recommend this manual!"

~ Catherine M. Lovett, PhD, ABD
Christian International Marketplace Administrator
Santa Rosa Beach, FL 32459, USA

■ ■ ■

"This manual reveals the secrets of Prophet Dr. Rohan Rambally's powerful ministry of signs, miracles and wonders. We are to look to Jesus and to minister to people as Jesus did! Prophet Dr. Rohan Rambally's manual has revolutionised the way in which I minister to people. I now minister to people by following the model of Jesus Christ. I use the commands and the decrees which are written in the Bible and which are outlined in full in this manual. The results have been amazing! Many people have been totally healed from physical, emotional and mental conditions after I have used the declarations and commands, which are clearly outlined in this manual! I highly recommend that everyone should read this manual in order to fully experience the resurrection power of Jesus in their own lives and in the lives of other people. Prophet Dr. Rohan Rambally has demonstrated that the ministry of Jesus is not complicated. This practical manual will change your perspective on the healing ministry of Jesus and it will enable you to experience the same resurrection power, which raised Jesus from the dead!"

~ Christine Korczak, Action Results Coaching
Leicester, England, United Kingdom

■ ■ ■

"If Jesus went about doing good and healing all that were in need, why wouldn't His followers do the same? Jesus is the same yesterday, today and forever!

The subject of divine healing is a very challenging one. Yet, in the Scriptures, we see that Jesus and the Early Church disciples functioned with an ability to heal the sick and to set the captives free by the commanding authority of the name of Jesus given to us at the Divine Exchange on the Cross. Often, there was a miracle of healing that happened before there was any opportunity to preach the Gospel - the healing opened the door, the Gospel was preached, and many lives were impacted for Jesus Christ.

'Divine Healing' is a key to the growth of the Christian Church - we must be a 'supernatural' Christian Church!

John 14:12 (NIV)...Very truly I tell you, whoever believes in me will do the works I have been doing, and they will do even greater things than these, because I am going to the Father.

For too long the church has done away with its God-given privilege of bringing freedom and deliverance to broken people. Dr. Rohan Rambally offers more than just a theology on divine healing, he includes many powerful testimonies with practical steps for you to become an instrument and a powerful vessel of Jesus' healing power by the authority you have as a believer of Jesus Christ. One of the testimonies depicted in this manual is my own husband's healing that took place in 2011 when he was miraculously healed of diverticulitis (a disease in the inner lining of the stomach tissues) , and prostate cancer at the same time by the use of commanding authority in Jesus name through Dr. Rambally. Today, my husband, Todd Smith is disease and cancer-free.

Dr. Rambally not only helped us to deepen our understanding of divine healing, but also shares from the grace to impart the same. I saw it even more first hand when we hosted Dr. Rambally and he spoke and demonstrated the power of God at our Shammah Outreach Ministries' Apostolic, Prophetic and Healing Encounter in Milton, ON – Canada in October of 2013. Many people got instantly healed including other cancer patients, heart patients, those with deaf ears, and the lame in walkers. Once the commands were given - they were all healed in Jesus' name! Cancer destroyed, heart patients running across the room with no issues, deaf ears opened and the lamed walked!

What has touched me the most about Dr. Rambally's powerful ministry of healing is the simplicity and practicality of his approach to this rather difficult subject. This should be a must-read for those who want to see God's healing power work for them and more so --- through them as believers of Jesus Christ.

Dr. Rambally's teachings have been imparted to us at Shammah Outreach Ministries and we are now commanding with authority and power and divine healings, miracles, signs, wonders, freedom and deliverance to the broken people are being manifested through us daily in Jesus' name.

Dr. Rambally's manual will elevate you from carnal limitations to the supernatural power -- unlimited!

The insights and remarkable personal accounts he shares will inspire your heart to not only walk in healing for yourself, but to be one who spreads God's healing power to others.

If you desire a better understanding of the authority within you as a believer of Jesus Christ and about divine healing, you'll find Dr. Rambally's manual insightful, instructive, and inspiring.

Through Dr. Rambally's profound biblical principles and teachings on divine healing, Shammah Outreach Ministries is flowing in the supernatural authority and power of Jesus Christ with the demonstration of healings, signs, wonders and creative miracles on a daily basis. This indeed is the supernatural Christian life!

Dr. Rambally's manual will convince you that healing is indeed for today!"

~ Sandra Benaglia Smith, Founder
Shammah Outreach Ministries
www.shammahoutreach.com

■ ■ ■

"Prophet Rohan combines intellect with Godly wisdom when writing this manual. He truly demonstrates how every believer can take hold of their God given authority to command divine healing and miracles in this present age. His anointed enlightenment of how Jesus operated in the 3 powerful offices of prophet, priest and king provide a clear concept of our Creator's life while on this earth and the legacy every believer can continue in.

Prophet Rohan exemplifies vividly yet with great simplicity and eloquence how all believers can operate in this same exact miraculous manner with the power of Christ. This publication is one that any child of God can benefit from and will most definitely be used as an excellent resource for generations upon generations to come."

Humbly Submitted

~ Dr. Tanya D. Mays- Jeune, FACOG, FMD
New York, U.S.A.

■ ■ ■

"This is a manual that all prophets and apostles need in order to have an impartation in their spirit, it is definitely chosen for the End time to release and unleash Yeshua's divine power and authority over sicknesses and demonic entities, and to release signs, wonders and miracles on the earth.

Myself and husband are Messianic believers of Yeshua with congregations in Europe and Jerusalem, and we have been impacted in the depth of our hearts with healings from Dr. Rohan Rambally.

Most importantly, his love impacted my ministry and my marriage in a great dimension.

His accuracy and flow of prophecy were in direct alignment with the word of Elohim, I decree and declare that Dr. Rohan Rambally will advance forward in divine kingdom authority over the nations as a king and heir to God and may Yeshua use him to expand the kingdom of God on the earth.

Thank you Prophet Rohan Rambally."

~ Prophetess and Apostle Nataliyah and David Malachi Jerusalem

■ ■ ■

"This manual flows out of the life and being of the author, Prophet, Dr. Rohan Rambally through the Holy Spirit who is vibrant in him. One of the most important elements is that the author not only has done his research but that the text flows out of His relationship with God and the Word.

This manual has you walking in the footsteps of Jesus and doing the greater works. It is a necessary tool in the arsenal of any believer to minister, to teach, to study, to activate, and learn how to flow in the miraculous.

It's a new wineskin of truth being restored to the Body of Christ. The manual blows the lid off of limitation and ignorance of not knowing our Kingly authority in Christ. It destroys the spirit of death, hell and the grave, the spirit of infirmity, sickness and disease, unbelief, and opens the throttle wide for the miraculous, for divine intervention, living in the supernatural and flowing by the Holy Spirit.

It is a must read and an on-going reference for strengthening and honing in regarding the responsibility and incredible opportunity we as believers have to disciple and equip the Church to do its work maximizing the tools and gifts we are endowed with from God.

In summation, having read this manual, I felt like I was born again, again, and I'm ready to do exploits. It will be revolutionary in its impact upon the church, thereby affecting the world at large through signs, wonders and miracles. I highly recommend that you read it, study it, and give to others to do the same for kingdom advancement until the King comes."

~ June Williams
Pastor/Chaplain
Maryland, USA

■ ■ ■

"This is a unique manual and you will find it very instructive. It is loaded with facts, very down to earth.It is a do-it-yourself kind of manual.In this manual,are insights that will help you to fight all oppositions,subdue the enemies,resist all intimidations until the best of God is manifest in your life."

~ Rev.S.Nnaka
Nigeria

■ ■ ■

"Prophet Dr. Rohan Rambally has penned together a manual that will shift the Body of Christ back to the basics in the realm of Divine Healing. This manual will clearly differentiate authority versus the gifts of healing. Anyone who puts into practice the activations outlined in these pages will see tremendous signs, wonders and miracles manifest in sync with the model of Jesus Christ and the early apostles. The keys in this manual will strategically align you in the realm of understanding your kingly authority and exercising divine authority to command healing in Jesus Name.

It is a must read for all believers!"

~ Bishop Hallam Harris
Apostolic Church of The West Indies
St. Michael, Barbados
West Indies

■ ■ ■

"How To Flow In The Miraculous is a manual that equips every believer on how to walk in their God-given authority to command healing in Jesus name. Therefore, having an in-depth understanding into the subject of healing is a requirement for everyone who wants to live in the realm of divine health as well as demonstrate it to their world. Dr. Rohan Rambally is a man with an unusual healing and prophetic anointing and has demonstrated the healing power of God in the lives of people across the nations of the world. He has released the secret of commanding your healing through this manual. This manual will inspire, encourage and motivate you to step out in faith and do what Jesus did by revealing His healing anointing to effectively communicate the message of salvation to mankind. I recommend every believer to get a copy of this manual."

Rev Chibuzor Ezekiel
Presiding Pastor
Jesus Foundation Family Intl, Manchester, UK

■ ■ ■

"I am very pleased to know that Dr. Rohan Rambally (led by the Spirit of God) has written about the subject of the Miraculous, particularly the area of Divine Healing.

Today, there are many persons suffering from diverse sicknesses all around us, visiting doctor after doctor searching for a permanent cure. But medical science does have its limits. This is real. Maybe it might be you the reader, a neighbor, family member or friend who needs healing from some form of disease. This manual schools the individual believer, step-by-step...teaching them how to confidently and accurately minister healing to the sick and witness the miraculous, healing power of God, almost instantaneously in many cases. 'How To Flow in the

Miraculous' will lead you into a dimension of the supernatural that very few have experienced; but which is available to us all, including you, as this manual rightly points out. Read it prayerfully, over and over again, until it is embedded in your spirit, and you too, begin to operate like Jesus the Messiah has commissioned and commanded you to, **Knowing that Healing the Sick is not Optional, it is Mandatory.**"

~ Roger Ali Bocus
President and Founder of the Literary Crusaders
Life-Coach, Entrepreneur & Motivational Speaker
Author of over 20 books

■ ■ ■

Dedication

This manual is dedicated firstly to my Lord and Saviour Jesus Christ, then to my entire family.

My beautiful mom and blessed dad who have stood by my side and encouraged me 100% to pursue the call of God as a prophet of the Lord to the nations. Without their support, love and encouragement I would not have been able to produce this manual for the Body of Christ.

I also dedicate this book to my two brothers Hamenath and Daren who have always been a tremendous blessing in my life, my sister-in-law Jessica who have assisted me with editing and the many hours invested in reviewing. Thanks to my two nephews, Luke and Matthias, who have continued to pray unceasingly for success in every facet of this Divine Healing Training Manual entitled "How To Flow In The Miraculous."

Acknowledgement

I can think of no better time than this to thank my spiritual sons and daughters who believed in me and gave of their time and talent to make this project a reality. Thank you for your prayers, faithfulness, and service, and because you understood that writing this manual was essential to the restoration of the ministry of the miraculous within the Body of Christ.

I would also like to acknowledge my course director and thesis supervisor Cathy Lovett of Christian International for her unending encouragement and help during my doctoral thesis/project/mechanics of research program. She constantly encouraged and motivated me in the right direction to get the thesis done according to international standards.

I would like to thank Brenda Sowder and the entire staff at Christian International for their constant love and support for the past seven years of nonstop study and work in spite of my constant itinerant prophetic ministry across the globe.

Thanks to Miss Karen Pegus for reviewing my thesis on its final release to Christian International School of Theology and thanks to Miss Ruth Ramsingh for her assistance in helping me to paraphrase certain sections of the training manual. A special thanks to Miss Carol Gray for reviewing the completed printed manual and for assisting me in having the necessary corrections done. A special thanks to my research assistant Matthew Dass for the countless hours he spent in research.

Thanks to Pastors Richard and Denique Alexander for reviewing my manual before its release and the countless hours of all night prayer which was spent by Pastor Richard interceding for the success of the material enclosed in this manual "How To Move in the Miraculous."

A special thanks to Mr. Roger Ali Bocus for his time, effort and energy exuded, and the countless hours of sacrifice which was made in order to get this manual published on time to be a blessing to the pastors in Guyana. A special thanks, as well, to his supportive family.

Thanks to all my friends locally and internationally for their prayers, love and support in every area, however small or big. Thank You and May the Lord bless you richly in Jesus Name.

How to Flow in the Miraculous

Divine Healing: Commanding
Your Healing In Jesus Name

By

Dr. Rohan Rambally

Table of Contents

Foreword

In his manual, 'How To Flow In The Miraculous,' Prophet Rohan Rambally has carefully disclosed and released the most powerful revelation of how to move, operate, live and flow in the miraculous.

His fresh, innovative and dynamic approach on moving in the miraculous allows you the reader the opportunity to learn how to command the healing power of the true and living God in a way never before made available in such a simple and layman format, that even the youngest believer in Christ can flow in miracles.

The secrets revealed in this manual through God's Prophet Rohan Rambally are priceless, in building and equipping the body of Christ to walk and flow in the miraculous like never before revealed.

"How To Flow In The Miraculous," will take you on a journey, where no man has gone before, deep into the realm of the spirit, and will clearly take you to a level of spiritual authority in Christ, that will enable and empower supernaturally the Body of Christ to walk daily in the miraculous.

If I had to choose one manual on performing miracles today, it would be, 'How To Flow In The Miraculous'.

Apostle Daren Rambally
Senior Pastor
Mc Bean House of Prayer
President & Founder of "Progress for Humanity"
Trinidad and Tobago

Preface

This manual was birthed through the encouragement from one of my best friends, Dr. Tyrone Dass to work on an area for my PhD Research, which initially was Prophetic Interpretation of Numbers. As a Mathematician, the Lord had given me the ability to translate the significance of numbers in our daily lives.

We sat for about three hours in my office, working on my proposal for my doctoral project. When he reached home, I received a call from him asking me why not shift to imparting what the Lord had been using me for at present and place it in a manual to be a blessing to the Body of Christ worldwide. This began the journey of this manual and its culmination into "How to Flow in the Miraculous."

For 17 years of my life, I operated in the prophetic office. I had received many prophecies that I would have flowed in signs, wonders and miracles. Even at a very early age in my walk with the Lord, I started praying for the sick. Sometimes I would spend anywhere from 5 minutes to 3 hours interceding for divine healing. Many individuals received their healing while others did not.

I questioned the Lord with respect to cancer, diabetes, arthritis and many other ailments as to what was the proper protocol to follow, in order that there be a manifestation of divine healing in the lives of people. It was also my greatest desire to be a medical doctor to help alleviate people's infirmities; however, I never knew God would use me strategically to heal the sick, raise the dead, cast out demons and perform miracles in Jesus Name.

I came in contact with my spiritual father Dr. Gary Greenwald in November, 2011 where he trained me in the area of creative miracles for realigning spines and bones in hands. At this point I saw 100% success in the realm of moving in the miraculous, new ligaments being re-created before my very eyes, damaged discs being recreated, scoliosis leaving within 5-30 seconds of prophetic declarations and prophetic healing manifested over and over again.

From that point onwards, the Lord placed an insatiable desire and hunger in me to learn even more. On January 2012, I had a dream of this gentleman called Pete Cabrera giving me a bunch of Divine Healing Training Manuals, so I decided to invite Pete Cabrera Junior to come and train us in the Prayer Command Centre to flow in the Miraculous for a three-day training Conference in the realm of Divine Healing on February17th - 19^{th,} of the same year. I witnessed deaf ears opening, skin conditions being healed and countless miracles. At the end of his stay, he gave to me, all of the manuals he had in his possession. He recommended that I study intensely, the Elijah Challenge Training by William Lau. On June 2012, I decided to invite Bro. William Lau and his wife to come to Trinidad and Tobago to teach us on how to flow in the miraculous. My life was changed forever because of the impact of his teachings which were based solely on the Word of God. They activated the Body of Christ in Trinidad on how to flow in the miraculous. They imparted into my life, the necessary training and equipment that I needed to propel me yet further in the realm of the miraculous.

At this point, I started seeing miracles beyond my wildest dreams, such as the following testimonial in our local church: A sound engineer had his entire finger cut off by machinery at his work place. I asked him if I can minister to him and he said yes. I commanded brand new cells, tissues, bones, flesh and a finger nail to come into being. As spoken, it was done in Jesus' Name within a month's time. Today, the gentleman has an entire member recreated by the power of the Holy Ghost.

Realizing the presence of the Holy Spirit's power resident within every believer, I decided to impart what the Lord had given me to others who were desirous to learn, grow and move in the realm of the miraculous. I started conducting Divine Healing seminars in churches and at other various venues. I began training nationals who would flow in the Spirit, thereby allowing the power of God to manifest the miraculous and thus bringing in the lost for Jesus Christ, as men see the mighty power of the Holy Ghost in action.

My goal is to properly educate the Body of Christ biblically with sound doctrine with respect to Divine Healing and shift the church into present day truths to equip you as a believer. This manual will be relevant to every other generation that will come, to enable them not only to read about the generals which we have had on the earth but that they themselves will rise up and come forth as a mighty army bringing forth healing and deliverance in their hands, speaking and commanding sicknesses and evil spirits to leave the bodies of men and women and seeing the miraculous explode at every angle on the earth.

My prayer is that everyone who comes into divine contact with "How To Move In The Miraculous," will start seeing instant healings and creative miracles. They would move in the realm of the supernatural by raising the dead. They would begin to cast out evil spirits with the Word of the Lord spoken out of their mouths. I pray that the Lord would impart spiritual gifts of healing as He did with Paul and Peter, that at your very shadow, that healings and deliverances would take place in the Name of Jesus. I pray that the power of the Holy Ghost would be so strong that you would be supersaturated with divine healing virtue. I pray that your hands will be blessed to release divine healing with everything that you touch, men and women would receive healing of every sickness and disease in the Name of Jesus. I pray the blessings of God upon your life. I pray as you study this manual, that you will be able to impart to others what you have learnt in this training manual that others would clearly understand proper spiritual protocol in the realm of divine healing and execute it effectively in the lives of people.

I pray that you would not revert to tradition but you would do as Jesus commanded in His Word and heal all those who are sick. I pray the Word of John 14: 12 "Verily, verily, I say unto you, He that believeth on me, the works that I do shall he do also; **and greater works than these shall he do**; because I go unto my Father."

I declare Numbers 6 : 24 -26 : "The Lord bless thee and keep thee : The Lord make his face shine upon thee, and be gracious unto thee: The Lord lift up his countenance upon thee, and give thee peace."

I declare the prayer of Jabez over your life according to 1 Chron. 4: 10 - "...Oh that thou wouldest bless me indeed, and enlarge my coast, and that thine hand might be with me, and that thou wouldest keep me from evil, that it may not grieve me!"

I release all that God has imparted into my life, into your divine destiny and declare that you will do exceedingly abundantly above all that you have asked or imagined to do, according to the power that worketh in you in the Name of Jesus. Amen and Amen.

Introduction

The hypothesis: Healing is accessible to everyone, even in the 21st century. Healing should be a regular practice of each believer in Christ to manifest God's healing power. For many years different Christian denominations have disagreed about healing and its relevancy today. Is God's miraculous healing still at work today, or did it die out when the apostles died?

Miraculous is defined as the supernatural intervention in the ordinary course of nature; an interruption of the system of nature as we know it. It is a supernatural manifestation by the Spirit that is sovereign by nature and not bound by any natural law. Miracles consist of acts of power such as raising the dead, producing water from a rock, and turning water into wine.

Divine healing sometimes called Faith Healing, is healing through spiritual / supernatural means. Believers say that a person may be healed by his/her religious faith through prayer or certain rituals that produce a divine presence and power that heals the disease and disability. Belief in divine intervention in illness or healing is related to religious belief. Faith Healing commonly refers to ritualistic practices of communal prayer and gestures (such as laying on of hands) that claim to invoke divine intervention and initiate spiritual and physical healing.

Throughout history, individual healers have claimed that healing for any illness, is possible through prayer and divine intervention, as well as ministration. Miraculous recuperations have been credited to many techniques commonly combined as "faith healing" which includes prayer, visiting a religious shrine, or an unwavering belief in a supreme being.

Faith healing is synonymous with Christianity. Very few interpret the Bible, especially the New Testament, as teaching belief in and practice of faith healing. The claims are that faith can cure blindness, multiple sclerosis, skin rashes, developmental disorders, anaemia, deafness, cancer, AIDS, total body paralysis, arthritis, corns, defective speech, and various injuries.

Many people have used the term "Divine Healing" without fully comprehending the true meaning of the term. The Bible tells us that healing is available to everyone.

Consistent manifestation of the miraculous power of God is based on several keys. Each of which will be clearly defined in this manual. Of these, the least understood and rarely practised is using our God-given authority in commanding healing. Every born again Christian believer has this authority and it is up to the believer to acknowledge and use it. It is one of the keys to witnessing miracles happen.

Jesus' Admonition to Go Forth and Heal

The Lord never once told us to pray for the sick. He told us to heal the sick. There is a big difference between the two. It has to do with operating in the authority that Jesus has already given to us. Look at these commands the Lord gave to His disciples:

"Then he called his twelve disciples together, and gave them power and authority over all devils, and to cure diseases. And he sent them to preach the kingdom of God, and to heal the sick." (Luke 9:1-2)

"And when he had called unto him his twelve disciples, he gave them power against unclean spirits, to cast them out, and to heal all manner of sickness and all manner of disease." (Matt. 10:1)

"And as ye go, preach, saying, the Kingdom of Heaven is at hand. Heal the sick, cleanse the lepers, raise the dead, cast out devils: freely ye have received, freely give." (Matt. 10:7-8).

The Lord has given us the power in our mouth to command. The Lord expects us to use that same authority in faith for healing to be manifested even today.

Chapter One

Three Offices of the Church in Administering Divine Healing

John Howard Reid discusses the three offices of the Church. Jesus Christ appeared two thousand years ago as priest, prophet and king. [1] After the Lord died and rose again, He returned to His Father in heaven, leaving the Church to complete the Great Commission. Christ had three offices, so too the Body of Christ on earth has been given three offices.

The Priestly Office

The priests of the Old Testament offered sacrifices to God on behalf of the sinful men. In an effort to completely atone for the entirety of man's sin, Christ offered His body as a blood sacrifice to God and thus fulfilled the role of the priests of old. In the New Testament, believers minister to God as priests but by offering slightly different sacrifices to Him. First of all, they offer their bodies to Him as living sacrifices (Rom. 12: 1). They offer to the Lord: praise, worship, thanksgiving, supplication and intercession (Ps. 100).

---

[1] Reid, John Howard. Prophet, Priest and King. Lulu Books. 2008. Pg.3

These are all priestly activities toward God. The priestly office is a very important part of the life of a believer. It is this very relationship a believer has with God that paves the way for the other offices. Without it, there would be no authority given to us, or a building up of wisdom and compassion (Jude 20). Everything in the priestly office is directed up to God such as supplication, prayer, worship, praise, fasting, etc.

The Prophetic Office

The primary function of a prophet is to prophesy to believers a word from God, whether it be a warning, for correction or to give direction. This is intended to strengthen, encourage, confirm and comfort as the disciples of Jesus Christ did (1 Cor. 14: 3). On occasion, they did speak forth God's word in a global sense, but the majority of times they ministered to the Body of Christ to build it up.[2] The prophetic office and prophetic activities are "horizontal" ministering as well as interacting with and forgiving fellow believers on earth (Mark 11 : 25,26).

The Kingly Office

The third office in which born-again believers are called to function is the kingly office. In Ecclesiastes, we read:

---

[2] Prophets and Personal Prophecy / Dr. Bill Hamon — Pg. 13, 14, quoted with permission. Copyright 1987-2014 CHRISTIAN INTERNATIONAL MINISTRIES. All Rights Reserved. www.christianinternational.com

Where the word of a king is, there is power; and who may say to him, "What are you doing?" (Ecclesiastes 8: 4).

Guillermo Maldonado in his book, The Kingdom of Power, says, "The Church of Christ is the only legal entity that can operate in God's supernatural power on earth."[3]

If believers are to emulate preaching the gospel with the authority and power as Jesus did, it is the kingly office that needs strengthening in their ministry.

Apostle Maldonado declares: "King Jesus does not need to answer to anyone; His supernatural presence and manifestations speak for themselves. The gospel of the kingdom has power because its message comes from the King Himself, who does not speak empty words, as men are prone to do; His words are full of authority and power. When we proclaim them, He confirms them with supernatural evidence by the Holy Spirit-the same Spirit who worked alongside Him during His ministry on earth." [4]

Although the kingly office can contain various activities, there is one aspect of this office which is vital to declaring the kingdom of God with power; the use of authority to enforce the rules set forth by Jesus.

---

[3] Maldonado, Guillermo. The Kingdom of Power. Whitaker House. 2013. Pg. 191
[4] Maldonado, Guillermo. The Kingdom of Power .Whitaker House. 2013. Pg. 151

The primary difference between a king and his subjects is that the king possesses authority over his subjects and not vice versa. The king uses his authority over them to execute his will and enforce his rules over the kingdom. The Israelite kings of the Old Testament waged wars against their enemy neighbours in order to bring to pass God's promise to Abraham and his descendants with regards to the Promised Land. Thus, the kingly office can be associated with spiritual warfare to destroy the works of the enemy (1 John 1: 10).[5]

Three common characteristics of all Kings:

• Kings possess authority to give commands. Because they possess authority, they do not need to ask or beg. (Ecclesiastes 8: 4)

• True kings are bold and courageous before their enemy. They do not cower in fear. (1 Tim. 1: 7)

• Kings have undeniable power to destroy their enemies or the works of their enemies. (Psalms 110: 1)

One prime example which can be cited as a man who walked in kingly authority was Lester Sumrall. The following testimony talks of how he understood his kingly authority and how he exercised his right as a child of God.

---

[5] Demolishing Demonic Strongholds / Dr. Morris Cerullo — Pg 242-244, quoted with permission. Copyright 2012-2014 MORRIS CERULLO WORLD EVANGELISM. All Rights Reserved. www.mcwe.com

PUT IT BACK - Lester Sumrall

"It is time for us to take back everything the devil has stolen from us. Prophetically, the time is right … and spiritually, the glory of the Lord is ready to come down like rain out of heaven … we must activate our faith into works! I realize you may not be fully aware how to use your faith and your authority against the forces of darkness that rule this world – you may not know how to claim back from the enemy what is rightfully yours in the spirit realm. So, here is a story that should help. Dr. Lester Sumrall years ago found himself in the middle of the Central American rain forest. As he went about his ministry in that region, he came across a witch doctor. In today's rock and roll Hollywood scene, this witch doctor would look like a normal man … but, in those days, this was a pretty strange fellow!

In one hand, the witch doctor would hold a bull frog (always a symbol of satanic power). In the other hand, a mixture of human blood and alcohol was placed in the frog's mouth. Then the witch doctor would dance, make satanic incantations and worship demon entities.

Fortunately, Dr. Sumrall wasn't raised in the modern-day school of humanistic, people-pleasing preachers. All Dr. Sumrall did was simply follow Jesus' biblical example. He placed his hands on the side of the witch doctor's head and said two words: Come out!

The witch doctor fell over with a thud. When he returned to his feet, the witch doctor was born again and speaking in a heavenly language and glorifying God.

Later, that night, Dr. Sumrall returned to his room to go to bed. Since it was warm, and without air conditioning, he decided to open the windows while he slept.

As he lay down, a strange odour began to fill the room. Suddenly, all of the sultry heat of the night disappeared from the room. A damp chill filled the place. It was so cold, Dr. Sumrall began to shiver. A wind began to blow the curtains wildly on their rods. Then, the bed began to shake so violently that it moved all the way out into the middle of the floor. Well, Dr. Sumrall had enough of this! He arose from his bed and said, "You demon spirit, I recognize you. I cast you out earlier today. In the name of Jesus Christ of Nazareth, you go now!" Immediately, the evil presence left the room. The heat returned. The curtains laid down against the wall, the bed stopped shaking. The horrible odour left the room. Dr. Sumrall rose back up in his bed, looked out the window and shouted, "Hey devil!

Get back in here!

Immediately the curtains began to stick out on end as a wind rushed through the room. The coldness returned ... the smell returned ... the bed began to shake violently and almost shook him out of bed. Dr. Sumrall sat up in his bed and said "Devil ... When I came into this room my bed was against that wall. Now, in the name of Jesus, PUT IT BACK!"

The bed went shaking back across the room and settled down against the wall. "Now," Dr. Sumrall ordered, "get out of here!" Today is the day of restoration for the church. We are not to be content with just making the devil leave ... but we are going to tell him to PUT IT BACK and restore EVERYTHING that he has stolen from us! This includes our healing. We have gathered our horses and sharpened our sword of God's Word. We have raised our banners and struck fear in the heart of our adversary ...

Now it is time to invade the enemy's territory and take back everything that rightfully belongs to us. The devil has the church's money ... the devil has the church's kids bound up on drugs ... the devil has taken away the church's health among its members ... and we are not going to wait for restitution any longer! We are going to get what is rightfully ours in the Lord!" [6]

Believers have this kingly authority to command. This authority did not die with the apostles. Surely it is time to be bold and strong and speak the Word of God in power.

---

[6] Devil put it back- The Refuge of Righteousness-(refugeofrighteousness.com)

Chapter Two

A History of Healing
and God's Conditions

It is important to ask the question, what is divine healing? Maria Woodworth-Etter in her book "Signs and Wonders" suggested, "Divine healing is the act of God's grace, by the direct power of the Holy Spirit, by which the physical body is delivered from sickness and disease and restored to soundness and health." [7]

Although illness is a matter of seriousness, its definition is simple; it is when the body fails to function normally. Myths and legends about divine healing do exist. Therefore, this will lead to an examination of the topic of "healing," both in the Old and New Testament of the Bible. In so doing, we will negate any misconceptions about the topic, such as the wrong view that few, if any Bible characters were gravely ill, or that they were healed quickly if they were seriously ill. Most importantly, we shall explore what exactly is the course of action or process of divine healing.

Healing In the Old Testament

Sickness and divine healing are mentioned a few times in the Old Testament, but are not really prevailing themes.

---

[7] Woodwood-Etter, Maria. Signs, and Wonders. Whitaker House.1997. Pg. 186

Old Testament references are put forward in the form of examples of illness, rather than doctrinal detailed discourses. This is a slight indication of the truth, that healing is not a strange and complex subject. If it were, we would not look forward to such few details of the subject.

An early mention of sickness is of Sarah's barren womb, (Gen. 17:17; 18:14), a problem that is still prevalent today, of women being infertile or barren. The healing that she received which resulted in the birth of Isaac in her old age is a well-known Bible story. Her womb's healing welcomed the ultimate spiritual healing of the world, through Jesus Christ, who was her descendant.

Sarah's experience teaches us that God's healing might not always be in our timing but can be delayed for a while in some cases, and that God had a purpose in her life that was beyond the physical, as he does in so many other lives. Christians acknowledge that all trials, not just sickness, serve a purpose in our lives, which goes beyond the physical and temporary.

Gen. 27:1 recounts how Isaac was blind for a number of years. Gen. 48:1-10 states that Jacob was "sick" and blind in his old age. They were not healed of these sufferings, something that is surprising to others who believe that righteousness is always and only equated with health or instant healing.

God clearly permitted extreme conditions of illnesses to not be healed, sometimes to bring individuals into His master plan. Exodus 15:26, mentions an important promise of God, about sickness and healing. The Lord said *"If thou will diligently listen to the voice of the Lord your God, and will do that, which is right in his sight, and will give ear to his commandments, and keep all his statutes, I will put none of these diseases upon you, which I have brought upon the Egyptians."* So here is a promise from God that He will not afflict with disease. The promise was for Israel if they would be obedient and it refers to not afflicting Israel with certain diseases, that God used to afflict Egypt.

Furthermore, in Exodus 23:23–25, God promises to take away sickness from the midst of the Israelites, if they obey Him and put Him first. Chapters 13 to 15 of Leviticus discuss the plague of leprosy and outline rules of isolation/quarantine. These chapters deny any claim that the children of Israel lived free from all illnesses or that they were always instantly healed. Likewise, Deuteronomy 7:15, compounds the promise that God will take away sickness upon the Israelites' obedience. Deuteronomy 32:39 is a confirmation that God heals ("I heal"). Deuteronomy 28:21–22, 60–61 declares illness as a curse for disobedience.

In 1 Kings 17:17–24, Elijah raises the widow's dead son, as evidence of God's power and mercy. The book of Job records Job's healing and his experience shows that sickness can befall even those who are living an upright and perfect life. It also shows how sickness is a real torment and torture to a person. The death of David's son, who was born out of adultery with Bathsheba, is also an example of illness without healing. Even though David was forgiven, the child still died. Another incident of illness is that of Elisha who became sick and eventually died from the illness. God then resurrected a dead man when the man's corpse came into contact with Elisha's bones. So it is plain to see that Elisha's death by sickness was no sign of unrighteousness. Then there is the healing of Hezekiah who was a righteous man. He got healed of an illness that God said would kill him (2 Kings 20:1–7). His pleading prayer to God and the extending of his life is evidence that God hears the prayers of those who obey him.

Healing In the New Testament

Quite different from the Old Testament, the New Testament contains numerous examples of mighty healings wrought by Jesus Christ. Although there were times when Christ healed simply out of his compassion (Matthew 20:24), His final purpose was much more universal. His healings were aligned with the preaching of the gospel. Matthew 9:35 states, *"Jesus went about all the cities and villages, teaching in their synagogues, preaching the gospel of the kingdom, and healing every sickness and every disease among the people."*

Christ went throughout Galilee teaching, preaching and healing all kinds of sicknesses and diseases (Matthew 4:23). Luke 6:17 tells of the large crowds, *"came to hear him and be healed of their diseases"*.

[48]

Isaiah's prophecy in the 53 rd chapter is confirmed in Matthew 8:17 and points out the words of Isaiah as a foretelling of the coming of Christ and His healing of the sick. The effect of Christ's healing of the sick would be to show the mighty power that the Messiah carried (Mark 3:15). By displaying His healing power, Jesus showed His power to forgive sin. Most of the times when He healed an individual, He pronounced forgiveness on that person. This is evidenced in the account of the paralytic man lowered through the roof, as told in Matthew 9, Mark 2 and Luke 5. A point to note is that most of Christ's healings were done publicly, but yet, were not meant for public attention. These healings were in effect, all immediate or nearly so (Matthew 15:21–31). The variety of people healed, were also broad, in terms of gender and age. Of some, Jesus demanded faith, (Matthew 9:29) of others, nothing was required. (Luke 7:11–17)

New Testament Examples

Maria Woodworth Etter implied, "Did Jesus heal everybody? Yes, all who came to Him in faith." "But they did not seem to have faith, did they? Yes." "At Nazareth, His own town, where He had been brought up, He could do no great work among them, 'because of their unbelief' (Matt. 13: 58). At Capernaum, where some of the most remarkable healings were wrought, the people were a believing people." [8]

Maria Woodworth Etter validated, "Didn't divine healing cease when Jesus finished His earthly ministry? No. It was more wonderfully manifested in the ministry of the apostles after the Day of Pentecost. See Acts 5 : 12-16; 3: 1-16 ; 14: 8-10; 9: 17-18; 8: 6-8 ; 19 : 11-12; 14 : 19-20; 9 :33-35 ; 36: 42; 20 : 8-12; 28 : 3-6,8. This proves clearly that divine healing is a redemptive blessing for the entire Holy Spirit dispensation. But we are taught that it was only for the beginning of the gospel dispensation. How about that? The Bible does not teach any such doctrine. But it does teach that 'when that which is perfect is come, then that which is in part shall be done away' (1 Cor. 13: 10). How about this? This Scripture has no reference to divine healing or any of the redemption blessings that they shall be done away with in this dispensation. If there ever has been a time in this dispensation when it could have been said with reference to the full possession and manifestation of the gospel blessings, that 'that which is perfect is come,' it was when the Holy Spirit came at Pentecost. But after this we see mighty works of salvation and healing, and they were in no sense done away with, but greatly increased. So you see the 'done away with'

---

[8] Woodwood-Etter, Maria. Signs, and Wonders. Whitaker House.1997. Pg. 186

argument has no scriptural basis whatever. As long as the dispensation of grace shall last, so long shall the benefits of grace be extended to 'whosoever will' (Rev. 22: 17). Well, then, when was divine healing done away? In the design of God it was never done away. Do you mean to say that it was perpetuated in the primitive church? Certainly it was. History shows it was perpetuated in the primitive church." [9]

In the New Testament, there were also examples of healing by the apostles. Acts 3: 1–16 tells of the case of the lame man who was healed by Peter and John. What is remarkable about this event is that the man was not even asking or expecting to be healed, but was simply begging for money. The apostle Peter also performed healings. Acts 5:15 says, *"They brought the sick out into the streets and laid them on beds and couches, that at least the shadow of Peter passing by, might fall on some of them."* In Acts 9:36–42, Peter heals Tabitha by raising her from the dead. Paul used handkerchiefs or aprons to perform great healings. (Acts 19:11–12) "Gifts of healing" are listed in 1 Corinthians 12:9–10, 28–30 among the spiritual gifts of Christians.

We see that even the apostle Paul experienced health problems from time to time (2 Corinthians 12:7). In spite of what we might expect, these servants of God were

---

[9] Woodwood-Etter, Maria. Signs, and Wonders. Whitaker House.1997. Pg. 186-187

not always healed. The book of James advises that when there are sick members among us, we must call for the elders of the church to pray for them.

> *"Is any sick among you? Let him call for the elders of the church; and let them pray over him anointing him with oil in the name of the Lord"* (James 5:14–15).

Series of Stages of Healing

Some of those who received healing had faith while others did not. Some, who got healed, were righteous, while others were not. Sometimes illnesses were a punishment from God but most times, it was just the result of physical causes or sin. Sometimes healings were instantaneous, sometimes they were delayed.

Divine healing is God's miraculous answer to the sick person's prayer. Since we see that illness is a trial like other trials and that divine healing is the answer to a person's prayer for relief or healing, other questions arise. Every time you are sick, does God promise to answer yes to your prayer for healing? Does He promise to do so immediately? Is healing a promise or is it simply an optional blessing from God?

Is Healing An Absolute Promise?

When James directs a sick person to call for the elders of the church and pronounces that the prayer of faith will save the sick, and the Lord will raise him up, such statement comes across as a promise. (See James 5: 14-15) Likewise, Psalm 103:3 states, *"Who forgives all your iniquities; who heals all your diseases."* Doesn't that sound like an absolute promise? There are numerous cases in the Bible where righteous persons became ill and were not healed. As was told earlier, Isaac and Jacob became blind in later years and Elisha died of an illness. The apostle Paul had an infirmity and it was not removed. So to say that God always heals every righteous person or every person who has faith, will contradict both scripture and our own experiences.

The Nature of God's Promise

Healing is a promise, as well as a wonderful blessing, which God gives in His good judgment. A promise is an "oral/written agreement to do or not to do something"[10]. So by its definition, many Bible statements about healing are certainly promises, because many statements say God will heal.

A promise can be conditional or unconditional. An unconditional promise is one in which the person who promises, will fulfil his promise without any action on the recipient's part. Therefore, if God promises to heal everyone, every time, immediately, then He has given an unconditional promise. A conditional promise however, is one to do or not to do something, but only if some action is

---

[10] Agnes, Michael E. The Webster's Dictionary. Wiley Publishing 2003. Quoted with permission. Copyright 2003-2014 John Wiley & Sons, Inc. All Rights Reserved. www.wiley.com

taken by another party. Hence, if God promises to heal us, only if we ourselves do something first, then God has made a conditional promise.

Healing Conditions

One condition for healing has long been that of faith or belief. In Matthew 9:29 it shows that faith was a condition for healing as Christ promised to heal if the person had faith. However, it is not to say that faith has always been a condition of healing, or that it necessarily must be every time God heals.[11] In the book of Acts 3:1-8, there was an example of healing where faith doesn't seem to be a factor. God has not bound himself to heal everyone who has faith. There is another condition whereby God heals on the condition that such healing is good for you, in terms of His overall plan for your life.

God's Will

Maria Woodworth Etter implied, "Just as you know that it is still God's will to save-by His Word. His Word is His will. But it may be His will not to heal me. You must go outside of God's Word to find standing ground for such a conclusion, for there is nothing inside of the Bible about healing but what corresponds with our blessed text: 'Himself took our infirmities and bare our sicknesses.'

---

[11]   Blake, Curry. Divine Healing Technician Training Manual. www.jglm.org. 2006. Pg. 39

(Isaiah 53:4) Most people argue that it might not be God's will to heal them are at the same time taking medicine and employing every possible human agency to get well. Why be so inconsistent? Why fight against God's will? If it is His will for you not to get well, then die. Stop fighting against God." [12]

God's purpose is to give you eternal life. God hears us whenever we ask anything in prayer, "according to his will."

"And this is the confidence that we have in him, that, if we ask anything according to his will, he heareth us." (1 John 5: 14)

Christians know that every prayer they pray in time of need is based on God's will and His overall view of what is in the best interest of the individual's life.

---

[12] Woodwood-Etter, Maria. Signs, and Wonders. Whitaker House.1997. Pg. 187

Chapter Three

Prophetic Office of Healing

The purpose of this chapter is to give present-day life experiences in personal prophecy, especially in relation to divine healing. In divine prophetic healing, the prophet is being used as God's mouthpiece to release healing into the individual. Ulf Ekman explains, "The prophet transfers something new into your life."[13] This flows along a horizontal direction into another individual's life.

Dr. Bill Hamon in his book, 'Prophets and Personal Prophecy' declares, "It is the prophetic word of a prophet which brings deliverance, healing, and creative miracles."[14]

What part can personal prophecy play in miraculous healings?

When the prophetic word of healing is released out of the mouth of a prophet or a prophetic person, it is like an arrow shot forth from the hand of the Almighty with precision and accuracy to hit the target. It is like the Almighty God Himself speaking, but, in this scenario He is

---

[13] Ekman, Ulf. The Prophetic Ministry. Word Of Life Publications. 1993. Pg. 209

[14] Prophets and Personal Prophecy / Dr. Bill Hamon — Pg 37, quoted with permission. Copyright 1987-2014 CHRISTIAN INTERNATIONAL MINISTRIES. All Rights Reserved. www.christianinternational.com

actually using someone on the earth to release His will of divine healing through prophecy.

Isaiah 55: 11 *"... So shall my word be that goeth forth out of my mouth: it shall not return unto me void, but it shall accomplish that which I please, and it shall prosper. ..."*

However, when the prophet of the Lord speaks, he is standing as the mouthpiece of God. When God speaks, His words go forth with divine power and authority to accomplish that which was spoken.

In the P.T.L. Study Guide it declares "goeth forth" [15] {[16]Strong's # [17]3318}. The Hebrew word "yatsa," is a verb which means to go or come out. The word of the Lord comes out of the prophet's mouth from the Lord and goes into the person's spirit, bringing change in the spiritual realm.

Prophetic miracles are manifested via these words which are spoken out of the mouth of seasoned prophets. Dr. Bill Hamon shares, "Probably ninety-nine percent of all

[15] Strong, James. P.T.L. Study Guide Strong's Concordance .PTL Television Network. 1976.Pg. 411

[16] Briggs, And C. Brown, F. Driver, S. THE BROWN-DRIVER-BRIGGS HEBREW and ENGLISH LEXICON. Hendrickson Publishers. 2008. Pg. 422 b

[17] Wigram, George V.THE ENGLISHMAN'S HEBREW CONCORDANCE OF THE OLD TESTAMENT. Hendrickson Publishers. 2006. Pg. 548 d

the healings and miracles I personally know about which happened through personal prophecy occurred when the one prophesying had no prior knowledge of the existing condition." [18]

A present day example of this occurrence was when I was invited to Scarborough, Ontario to do a Prophetic Healing Conference. In 2011, I prophesied that Todd Smith would be healed of prostate cancer, spinal pains and diverticulitis and as a sign that the Lord was healing him; he would experience the burning fire of God over his body. Todd declared that he joyfully went home from the meeting that night. He was all happy that he had received this prophetic word, however, at midnight he got up screaming. He shared that his whole body was on fire. His wife got alarmed and asked if he needed to go to the doctor.

He remembered the prophetic word spoken by me. The next day he went to his oncologist and when the doctor checked his PSA level it was radically reduced. He then went to his chiropractor and his spine was perfectly aligned. Lastly, he was able to eat nuts, and the sesame seed Big Mac bun from Mac Donald's without any bowel issues.

---

[18]Prophets and Personal Prophecy / Dr. Bill Hamon — Pg. 42, quoted with permission. Copyright 1987-2014 CHRISTIAN INTERNATIONAL MINISTRIES. All Rights Reserved. www.christianinternational.com

After six months, he revisited the oncologist and he was in perfect health with a normal PSA level. He told the doctor he believed the Word of the Lord and he will not be seeing him again. Up to this present day Todd is walking in perfect health and strength and giving God all the glory for the prophetic word which was spoken by me.

This is a second testimonial of a prophetic healing which was done in Milton, Ontario at the Best Western Ballroom on October 13th, 2013. Quote from the e-mail from Allîançâ Shellé & Christopher as follows: "It seems hard to believe it was almost one week ago since you prophesied over us. I actually went to see the neurologist this past Thursday Oct 17 and as you said, "I'M HEALED." After examining me for 35 minutes the doctor concluded, he could not find anything wrong with me and encouraged me to continue living my life and in time the symptoms will dissipate."

A third manifestation of prophetic healing was given to Lynette Rouse. A direct quote from her e-mail as follows: "Monday 21st October, 2013, "My mom had sore, swollen feet, and dark, smooth, dry hands that were almost insensitive to touch which was a side effect from the cancer treatment. Prophet prayed. He called forth healing. Before our eyes we saw the swelling in mom's feet recede. Her skin began to regain its natural colour and her tendons which we have not seen for months became visible. Hallelujah! He prophesied that in two to three weeks her hands will regain their colour as well and thus far, it is happening. " And, "Earlier this year we received positive reports from the doctor who said that some cancer cells that were present in her lungs are gone."

In conclusion, prophetic praying and personal prophecy, when divinely directed, brings miraculous results within those who receive the ministry of the prophet.[19]

---

[19] Prophets and Personal Prophecy / Dr. Bill Hamon — Pg 37-49, quoted with permission. Copyright 1987-2014 Christian International Ministries. All Rights Reserved. www.christianinternational.com

Chapter Four

Kingly Office

In the New Testament, we read in Rev 1: 5-6:

"To [Christ Jesus] who loved us and washed us from our sins in His own blood, and has made us kings and priests to His God and Father..."

It is the destiny of each and every believer to step into their kingly role and function.[20]

Who is a King?

Dr. Cindy Trimm postulates, "A king has the legal power to decree, which is an old English word for "Legislate." He institutes, he confirms, he settles, he summons, he authorizes, that is what a king does."[21] Apostle Maldonado in his book, "The Kingdom of Power" says, "...everyone of his people is a king and a priest, created to take dominion over his assigned territory with the authority and power God delegated to him to extend His reign on earth." [22]

---

[20] Destined to Reign / Joseph Prince — Pg. 1, quoted with permission. Copyright 2007-2014 Harrison House. All Rights Reserved. www.harrisonhouse.com

[21] Trimm, Cindy. Commanding Your Morning. Charisma House. 2007 Pg. 40

[22] Maldonado, Guillermo. The Kingdom of Power. Whitaker House.2013. Pg. 207

Believers must recognize that God has called them forth to walk in their kingly authority and power. Our King Jesus has left believers a perfect picture of divine authority with the miraculous works that He accomplished on the earth and yet greater works shall His kings on this earth do in His mighty Name.

Kings have a legal right to exercise power and dominion over the sphere of influence in which they rule. They have the legal right to effect changes on the earth as God acts in heaven and for His divine will to be done on the earth through the power of the Holy Ghost. God has called the Church to rule with the rod of authority.

"The LORD shall send the rod of thy strength out of Zion: rule thou in the midst of thine enemies.

Thy people shall be willing in the day of thy power, in the beauties of holiness from the womb of the morning: thou hast the dew of thy youth." (Psalm 110: 2-3)

The Hebrew word for rod is "matteh" or "mattah" and the most appropriate meaning is a "sceptre."[23] In other words, God has placed a sceptre of His authority in our hands and has given us the legal right to rule and reign with Him here and now on the earth.

---

[23] Thayer, Joseph H. Thayer's Greek-English Lexicon of the New Testament. Hendrickson Publishers. 2007. Pg. 540

God is not going to come down from Heaven and release this divine authority. This authority has already been released into our hands.

It is up to the Body of Christ to rise up and walk in their divine authority as kings upon the earth.

> *"Wherefore God also hath highly exalted him, and given him a name which is above every name: That at the name of Jesus every knee should bow, of things in heaven, and things in earth, and things under the earth; And that every tongue should confess that Jesus Christ is Lord, to the glory of God the Father."* (Phil. 2: 9 -11)

> *"Having therefore, brethren, boldness to enter into the holiest by the blood of Jesus."* (Heb. 10: 19)

The authority is in the Name of Jesus Christ[24]. The Body of Christ has been given the Name that is above every other Name. In the Name of Jesus Christ believers have access to enter boldly into the very Holy of Holies. Believers must come boldly and walk in their divine authority in the realm of their kingly office.[25] All subjects in earth and under the earth must be subjected to that

---

[24] Lord Teach us to Pray/ Dr. Morris Cerullo – Pg. 227 – 228, quoted with permission. Copyright 2004-2014 Morris Cerullo World Evangelism. All Rights Reserved www.mcwe.com

[25] Lord Teach us to Pray/ Dr. Morris Cerullo – Pg. 229, quoted with permission. Copyright 2004-2014 Morris Cerullo World Evangelism. All Rights Reserved www.mcwe.com

powerful, majestic, glorious name of Jesus. According to Smith Wigglesworth, "There is power to overcome everything in the world through the name of Jesus."[26]

The Name of Jesus must be used at all times to access all realms and to open all doors in the spirit. Just the mention of the Name of Jesus is sufficient to cause breakthroughs to take place in the spirit. As kings we must first understand the power that lies locked up in that Name.[27]

Kings must understand that everything is accessible to them in Heaven and on earth through the Name of Jesus. The early apostles understood the authority in the Name of Jesus to unlock healing.

> "Then Peter said, *Silver and gold have I none; but such as I have give I thee: In the name of Jesus Christ of Nazareth rise up and walk. And he took him by the right hand, and lifted him up: and immediately his feet and ankle bones received strength."*)

Peter then confirmed it was not by his holiness or his power that had made the lame man at the Gate Beautiful whole. It was only through faith in the Name of Jesus.

---

[26] Wigglesworth, Smith. Healing. Whitaker House.1999. Pg. 13
[27] Lord Teach us to Pray/ Dr. Morris Cerullo – Pg. 229 – 230, quoted with permission. Copyright 2004-2014 Morris Cerullo World Evangelism. All Rights Reserved www.mcwe.com

"And his name through faith in his name hath made this man strong, whom ye see and know: yea, the faith which is by him hath given him this perfect soundness in the presence of you all."(Acts 3: 16)

Authority Delegated to us

".speak the word only and my servant shall be healed."(Mat. 8: 8)

Jesus Christ "spoke the word" and miracles, signs and wonders took place. Kings must likewise speak the word only and manifest the same miracles, for whatever King Jesus says, we may also boldly say. This is confirmed by Dr. Morris Cerullo:

"Jairus, the ruler of the synagogue, came to Jesus and said, "My little daughter is sick."Jesus said, "I will come to your house and I will heal her." By the time Jesus got to Jairus' house, the girl was dead and Jesus and Jairus were met by mockers who laughed them to scorn. Jesus put them all out. Jesus took the little girl by the hand and said, "Damsel, I say unto thee, arise!" He spoke the Word...Divine Authority.

Speak the Word!

The child's body was there but her spirit was not. Her spirit already had left her body and had travelled down the corridor of time. When Jesus spoke the words, "Damsel, I say unto thee, arise!"

in obedience to the word and the authority of Jesus Christ, her spirit turned right around and came right back into her dead body. She got up out of that bed, resurrected, because Jesus spoke the Word!

Speak the Word!

Speak the Word!

Speak the Word!

...he hath said, I will never leave thee, nor forsake thee. So that we may boldly say, The Lord is my helper, and I will not fear what man shall do unto me." (Hebrews 13: 5-6)[28]

Our King never prayed for a sick person.[29] He was a Man of Authority. **He simply spoke the Word!**

He released decrees, declarations and proclamations in the spirit. He simply spoke the word! Likewise, His believers must simply speak the word. The Lord Jesus Christ did not just give believers responsibility without giving them divine authority to execute that divine responsibility.

---

[28] THE NEW PROOF PRODUCERS / Dr. Morris Cerullo – Pg 216 & 217, quoted with permission. Copyright 1988-2014 Morris Cerullo World Evangelism. All Rights Reserved. www.mcwe.com
[29] THE NEW PROOF PRODUCERS / Dr. Morris Cerullo – Pg 209, quoted with permission. Copyright 1988-2014 Morris Cerullo World Evangelism. All Rights Reserved. www.mcwe.com

"But ye shall receive power, after that the Holy Ghost is come upon you: and ye shall be witnesses unto me both in Jerusalem, and in all Judaea, and in Samaria, and unto the uttermost part of the earth." (Acts 1: 8)

King Jesus has given the Church the responsibility of bearing witness to Himself throughout the length and breadth of the universe. He has also released upon the Body of Christ His divine authority to execute this task.

As kings, believers are subject to the King of the Universe. They are subject to His voice and His call to fulfil His divine will upon this earth. His Kings have the same ability to speak His word out of their mouths and it like exactly as if it is God's Word in His mouth being spoken forth.

Dr. Atkins, in his book, defines DNA as follows: **"Deoxyribonucleic acid (DNA)** is a molecule that encodes genetic information in the nucleus of a cell and determines its structure, function, and behaviour."[30]

As kings, believers carry the exact spiritual DNA of the King of Kings and the Lord of Lords. The DNA within every born again believer is royal DNA that flows from the

---

[30] Atkins, C. Robert, Vernon C. Mary & Eberstein A. Jacqueline. Atkins Diabetes Revolution. William Morrow : An Imprint of HarperCollins Publishers, 2004.

throne of Jesus Christ. The divine nature and attributes of the spiritual code which enabled Jesus Christ to perform signs, wonders and miracles is embedded within the believer's spiritual man. The Healer and Miracle Worker is alive in every child of God by virtue of the blood of Jesus which flows into your veins as a born again believer. This is confirmed by Morris Cerullo:

> "God created man in His image because He wanted to reproduce Himself. God's image in us, God's image in humanity..."[31]

All that Christ miraculously accomplished, while He was on the earth is available now in this present time and season to every child of God. It is important to realize the residential power and authority that is embedded in the spirit of His children. It is very important that believers are first taught, trained, equipped and mentored in the kingly office in order to function in dominion and power.

The Blood Covenant and the Kingdom

> *"And from Jesus Christ, who is the faithful witness, and the first begotten of the dead, and the prince of the kings of the earth. Unto him that loved us, and washed us from our sins in his own blood, And hath made us kings and priests unto God and*

---

[31] THE NEW PROOF PRODUCERS / Dr. Morris Cerullo – Pg. 126, quoted with permission. Copyright 1988-2014 Morris Cerullo World Evangelism. All Rights Reserved. www.mcwe.com

his Father; to him be glory and dominion forever and ever. Amen." *(Revelation 1: 5-6)*

"And they sung a new song, saying, Thou art worthy to take the book, and to open the seals thereof: for thou wast slain, and hast redeemed us to God by thy blood out of every kindred, and tongue, and people, and nation; And hast made us unto our God kings and priests: and we shall reign on the earth." (Revelation 5: 9-10)

Through the blood of Jesus Christ, believers have become "kings and priests" to their loving Heavenly Father. As King Jesus promoted justice and the ways of God in the earth, believers are to follow in their King's footsteps.

The Kingdom of God is totally different from the natural kingdoms in the earth realm and operates by different laws. In England, you must be born into or marry someone in order to be part of the royal family, however in the Kingdom of God, one must be born again by the Holy Spirit. The only way an individual can become a citizen of the Kingdom of God is being born into it, but not through the natural means.

"Marvel not that I said unto thee, ye must be born again." (John 3: 7)

Jesus further cements His divine purpose about the role of his death which would be integrated in the salvation and entrance into God's everlasting Kingdom.

> *"Then Jesus said unto them, Verily, verily, I say unto you, except ye eat the flesh of the Son of man, and drink his blood, ye have no life in you. Whoso eateth my flesh, and drinketh my blood, hath eternal life; and I will raise him up at the last day. For my flesh is meat indeed, and my blood is drink indeed. He that eateth my flesh, and drinketh my blood, dwelleth in me, and I in him."* (John 6: 53-56)

From the perspective of the 'Lord's supper,' His children must have an intimate relationship with Him through the blood sacrifice where we can enter boldly before the throne of the Lord.

> *"Having therefore, brethren, boldness to enter into the holiest by the blood of Jesus."* (Hebrews 10: 19)

> *"They overcame him by the blood of the Lamb and the word of their testimony and they loved not their lives unto the death."* (Rev. 12: 11)

The royal blood of Jesus flows through our veins. Believers must also understand that there is power in the blood of Jesus. The blood of Jesus breaks all curses and chains in the spirit realm.

"Christ hath redeemed us from the curse of the law, being made a curse for us: for it is written, Cursed is every one that hangeth on a tree." (Gal 3: 13)

Mary K Baxter writes in her book, The Power of the Blood,

"One day, the Spirit of God spoke to me and told me to go to the children's hospital to pray for someone. I didn't know anyone who was admitted to that hospital, but I obeyed the Lord. His spirit led me down a hallway to where I heard a child crying. I entered the child's room and tried to comfort him. Jesus said to me, 'Lay your hands on his stomach and plead My Blood covenant over him. I obeyed the Lord, and the child went to sleep. The doctors did more X-rays and found that the little boy was completely healed. The blood of Jesus Christ had done its work." [32]

"He was wounded for our transgressions, He was bruised for our iniquities; the chastisement for our peace was upon Him, and by His stripes we are healed." (Isaiah 53: 5)

Answer the Call to Be a King

---

[32] Baxter, Mary K. The Power of the Blood, Whitaker House. 2005. Pg. 173, 174

"But ye are a chosen generation, a royal priesthood, a holy nation, a peculiar people; that ye should shew forth the praises of him who hath called you out of darkness into his marvellous light." *(1 Peter 2: 9)*

God has specifically chosen and ordained those who would repent and turn to Him to be a part of His Kingship on the earth. It is only according to His purpose and grace. (See 2 Tim. 1: 9) Jesus died for this divine purpose that men and women will be washed, cleansed and redeemed by His blood so that they will emulate His Kingly authority in the earth.

"For we know that the whole creation groaneth and travaileth in pain together until now. And not only they, but ourselves also, which have the first fruits of the Spirit, even we ourselves groan within ourselves, waiting for the adoption, to wit, the redemption of our body." *(Rom. 8: 22 -23)*

King Jesus always spoke the desired result while He was on the earth and likewise His 'kings' of today must do the same. Kings must use their rod of authority in the environment they have been strategically assigned to by the King of Kings. His kings must take authority over all sickness in people's bodies and heal them.

Chapter Five

Royal Gifts to the Body of Christ

"Wherefore he saith, when he ascended up on high, he led captivity captive, and gave gifts unto men. (Now that he ascended, what is it but that he also descended first into the lower parts of the earth? He that descended is the same also that ascended up far above all heavens, that he might fill all things.)

And he gave some, apostles; and some, prophets; and some, evangelists; and some, pastors and teachers; For the perfecting of the saints, for the work of the ministry, for the edifying of the body of Christ: Till we all come in the unity of the faith, and of the knowledge of the Son of God, unto a perfect man, unto the measure of the stature of the fulness of Christ."(Eph. 4: 8-13)

God has chosen to give to His beloved children "gifts" from on high. These gifts are spiritual gifts from the throne of the Lord. The Lord has earmarked His kings upon this earth to receive these gifts to be a blessing to mankind. The gifts are for the purpose of equipping the body of Christ for the work of the ministry. The Lord has strategically assigned His five-fold gifts: to impart, teach, train, equip and disciple His army into present truth to fulfil all He has ordained, planned and purposed to come forth on the earth.

In order for the gifts of the spirit to be effective the Church needs a strong and proper foundation, on the rock. A church built on divinely chosen Apostles and Prophets has a strong foundation that will last and the "gifts of the spirit" can move in an effective and unrestricted manner. [33]

Gifts of Healing Dispensed To the Body of Christ

"Now there are diversities of gifts, but the same Spirit. And there are differences of administrations, but the same Lord. And there are diversities of operations, but it is the same God which worketh all in all. But the manifestation of the Spirit is given to every man to profit withal. For to one is given by the Spirit the word of wisdom; to another the word of knowledge by the same Spirit; To another faith by the same Spirit; to another the gifts of healing by the same Spirit; To another the working of miracles; to another prophecy; to another discerning of spirits; to another divers kinds of tongues; to another the interpretation of tongues: But all these worketh that one and the selfsame Spirit, dividing to every man severally as he will." (1 Corinthians 12: 4-11)

"To profit withal" here is understood to be for the good of the *body of Christ*. All nine gifts of the Holy Spirit therefore are primarily for ministering to believers in the

---

[33] Training Manual ESTHER PROJECT volume 3 / Tomi Arayomi – Pg. 28, quoted with permission. Copyright February 6, 2011-2014. All Rights Reserved Tomi Arayomi Ministries.

body of Christ. In particular, the "gift of healing" is for ministering to infirm believers in the context of building up the body of Christ.

Gifts of Healing

William McRae defines the gift of healing as follows: "The ability to heal diseases, any and all diseases, miraculously is possessed by the person with the gift of healings." [34]

There is no scriptural evidence to prove that the gift of healing ceased with the death of the apostles, this is confirmed by Dr. Terrance Jenkins, "I am persuaded that the day of miracles have not passed away, but are still here because the God of miracles is still present and have not changed. All it takes is faith in God." [35]

The gift of healing refers to the supernatural ability to heal people of physical diseases in response to: the laying on of hands, praying in Jesus' name or a combination by the person through whom the Spirit wills to channel the gift (Acts 3:2, 6-8; 14:8-10). [36]This is done for

---

[34] Taken from Dynamics of Spiritual Gifts by William Mc Rae Copyright © 1976 by Lamplighter Books. Pg. 69 Used by permission of Zondervan. www.zondervan.com
[35] Nineteen Gifts of God to His Children, by Dr. Terrence Jenkins, p.84. Copyright 1991, 48 HrBooks. Used by permission.
[36] THE NEW PROOF PRODUCERS / Dr. Morris Cerullo – Pg 209, quoted with permission. Copyright 1988-2014 Morris Cerullo World Evangelism. All Rights Reserved. www.mcwe.com

the building or edification of the ailing members of the body of Christ. In (1 Corinthians 12:9, 28, 30), Paul includes "gifts of healing," in his list of spiritual gifts given to the believers. 'Gifts,' not 'gift', of healing is mentioned in the plural form without the definitive 'the.' This indicates that healing is Holy-Spirit-given as well as a transient or occasional gift. In other words, healing is a gift that can be exercised by a person according to the will of God. This gift is not permanent or even 100% successful with any one person to hold the title "Faith Healer." Even Paul, who healed many, was unable to heal Epaphroditus (Phil 2:25-30). Also, according to Smith Wigglesworth, the gifts of healing go hand in hand with long suffering in a cause-effect sort of relationship, each dependent on each other and activating each other. [37]

In the Bible, it appears that Jesus alone was able to heal every time. Note that the Bible does allow the work of a physician and the use of modern day medicinal care. (Matt 9:12; Luke 10:34; Col 4:14; 1 Timothy 5:23)

Before closing this chapter, I must add that although all believers are commanded to lay hands on the sick and command healing into their body, and they shall recover – This is the general command to all believers by our Lord Jesus Christ; it is believed that not all believers have the 'Gifts of Healing' operational through them. The 'Gifts of Healing has to do with special anointings given to certain

---

[37] Wigglesworth, Smith. Smith Wigglesworth on Healing. Whitaker House. 1999. Pg. 142

individuals to heal specific kinds of sicknessess. For instance, some people who have operated in the 'Gifts of Healing' have claimed to have had more success with praying for lame people, others see more blind persons healed in their ministry than any other sickness...

But whether you have the 'Gifts of Healing' functional through you or not, you are commanded by the Lord Jesus Christ to command healing into sick bodies and they shall recover. Just do what you have been commanded to do, and if the Lord decides to allow the 'Gifts of Healing' to operate through you, then so be it.

It is the Spirit of God who decides who He wants to give the 'Gifts of Healing' to – whether that is you or someone else.

Chapter Six

The "How"Of Healing

How Does God Heal?

"God healed through **natural substances** from the knowledge He has imparted to man. This includes the skill of physicians and surgeons but also includes alternative approaches to healing! God also heals through **miracles**. How often physicians have seen a healing take place they cannot understand. Some refuse to accept it as miraculous healing by God. Instead they call it a "remission" of the disease. In some cases, that healing is **instantaneous**. In other cases scripture tells us that the healing was **progressive**."[38] Salem Kirban. (2 Kings 5:10)

How Did Jesus Heal?

Jesus Being Anointed By The Holy Spirit Caused The Following:

"And came down to Capernaum, a city of Galilee, and taught them on the Sabbath days. And they were astonished at his doctrine: for his word was with authority." (*Luke 4: 31, 32*)

---

[38] Kirban, Salem. How To Discover Abundant Health and Happiness Following God's Guidelines. SECOND COMING INC. 2000. Pg. 80

The word authority is translated "exousia" in the Greek which simply means the power to act. It is also the right or privilege to exercise delegated empowerment.[39]

At His Baptism, Jesus was anointed by the Holy Spirit and given authority. He demonstrated this authority in a way that amazed people. Maldonado comments as follows: "The authority of the kingdom gives the legal right to exercise God's power."[40] Examining the nature of this authority and how Jesus exercised it is the key for His kings to flow in apostolic authority likewise.

> "And in the synagogue there was a man, which had a spirit of an unclean devil, and cried out with a loud voice, Saying, Let us alone; what have we to do with thee, thou Jesus of Nazareth? Art thou come to destroy us? I know thee who thou art; the Holy One of God." (Luke 4: 33, 34)

During Jesus' teachings in the local synagogue, there was a sudden commotion. In the presence of the Lord a demon manifested in a man, and he shouted involuntarily under the demon's influence. For individuals who have never seen a demonic manifestation, it may be a terrifying experience. How did Jesus deal with the situation?

---

[39] Thayer, Joseph H. Thayer's Greek-English Lexicon of the New Testament. Hendrickson Publishers. 2007. Pg. 225

[40] Maldonado, Guillermo. How to walk in the Supernatural Power of God. Whitaker House. 2011. Pg. 234

As a king, believers must follow what the King of Kings did in this situation.

"And Jesus rebuked him, saying, Hold thy peace, and come out of him!" (Luke 4: 35)

Did Jesus pray for the demon possessed man or ask the Father to set him free? No, Jesus instead commanded the demon to be silent and to leave the man.

• Did Jesus say: Father, we command this evil spirit to be silent and to depart from him? No, Jesus did not communicate with his Father, but rather he spoke directly to the demon.

• Do you think Jesus had his eyes closed? There is no biblical evidence or reason to suggest that Jesus closed his eyes while issuing a command to the demonic entity.

• Was there any prophetic or priestly component such as prayer, prophecy or thanksgiving to the Father in Heaven? No, the response was absolutely kingly in nature in direct alignment of a command directed to the evil spirit.

Why did Jesus not involve the Father in the deliverance of the man? Being anointed with the Holy Spirit meant that He received authority over demons from His Father. This authority enabled Jesus to drive out the demon. The demon was subjected to His authority; it was compelled to obey Jesus' command.

"And when the devil had thrown him in the midst, he came out of him, and hurt him not." (*Luke 4:35*)

How did Jesus bring about this miracle? The miracle was performed by executing the authority given by the Father to Jesus. Authority is not executed by praying, but by commanding.

"And they were all amazed, and spake among themselves, saying, what a word is this! For with authority and power he commandeth the unclean spirits, and they come out" (*Luke 4:36*)

The people were astonished at what Jesus said in His words. What words? The words were, *"Be quiet, and come out of him."* Why were these words so amazing to the observers?

Jesus Christ possessed authority and power over evil spirits just as God does. The evil spirit obeyed His every command and left the man. Who was this miracle working man?

As Jesus was anointed by the Holy Spirit at the Jordan River, He received divine authority over demons from His Heavenly Father. He exercised authority not by praying to His Father, but by commanding evil spirits to leave. It must be noted, here is a foundational principle that should be obvious to anyone.

If believers have authority over something or someone, they must exercise that authority not by praying, but by *commanding*. [41]Cindy Trimm implies, that the meaning of the word command is, "to order with authority; to take charge of; to exercise direct authority over; to lead; to dominate by position; to guard; to overlook." Not once did Jesus go out into the frontlines to pray for the sick, He simply decreed, declared and commanded and it was done. The only instance where Jesus spoke to His Heavenly Father recorded in the Scriptures was with Lazarus when He raised him from the dead. (John 11: 38 -44)

How Did Jesus Deal With Physical Ailments?

It is important to distinguish between physical infirmities and infirmities inflicted by evil spirits. Physical infirmities are not intelligent entities which can hear and understand. Therefore an individual cannot rebuke command or speak to them any more than one can talk to an object like a rock. [42]

In the church, believers are taught that when someone has a purely physical infirmity, all that can be done is pray for that individual through intercession for the Lord's will to be done in His time. Many believers seek the help of physicians, which is fine. However, it is very important to follow the King and how He ministered to the

[41] Trimm, Cindy. Commanding Your Morning. Charisma House. 2007 Pg. 113

[42] Maldonado, Guillermo. Jesus Heals your sickness today. ERJ Publications.2009. Pg. 53

physically infirmed and ask questions concerning the method which He used in order for His kings in this present hour to flow in His delegated authority.

Did He intercede to the Father for their healing?

> *"Jesus left the synagogue and went to the home of Simon. Now Simon's mother-in-law was suffering from a high fever, and they asked Jesus to help her. So he bent over her and rebuked the fever, and it left her."* (Luke 4:38, 39)

• Did Jesus intercede for her? No, He did not.

• Did Jesus say: "Father, we command this fever to leave?" No. Many believers of charismatic and Pentecostal persuasion are often trained to minister this way to the physically infirm as seen in Apostle Maldonado's book.[43] But Jesus never included His Father during the act of ministering to the sick.

• Did Jesus shut his eyes? No, there is no biblical evidence to support that claim. Some believers have developed a habit of closing their eyes when ministering to the sick.[44]

---

[43] Maldonado, Guillermo. Jesus Heals your sickness today. ERJ Publications.2009.Pg 190

[44] Hudson, Virginia Cary. Close your eyes when praying. New York: Harper & Row Hudson, 1968

- Was there any priestly factor such as praise or worship to the Father? No, the action was absolutely kingly in nature, purely a direct command to the fever.

How did Jesus bring about this miracle? He healed the woman simply by rebuking the fever in the same way as He had rebuked the demon in the man at the synagogue. Jesus commanded the fever to leave the woman, and it obeyed His directive. From this we can conclude that when Jesus was anointed by the Holy Spirit at the Jordan River, He received divine authority not only over evil spirits but over physical maladies as well.

Demons have the ability to hear, understand and respond to spoken commands. How could Jesus communicate to the fever?

It's All about Authority

According to Dictionary.Com, Authority is defined as: "The power to determine, adjudicate, or otherwise settle issues or disputes; jurisdiction; the right to control, command, or determine."[45]

"There's a progression of authority that begins with God the Father, passes on to Christ the Son, then to his disciples, and finally to us." [46] Mahesh Chavda.

---

[45]   N.P.,   N.A.   N.D.   Dictionary.com.   < http://dictionary.reference.com/browse/authority>

For example, a pet that is under the owner's authority will always submit to the owner's command, whatever that command may be. Furthermore, with young children who are under the authority of their parents; when they are misbehaving the parents will correct them. Parents do not need to go to God with a prayer to subdue an unruly child; the parents have the authority within themselves to discipline the child whenever they misbehave. When children become parents they are now entrusted with the same parenting authority as their parents.

Although, a pet and a child are very different, they are similar in some ways, in that they both are under the authority of the parents/owner and must be obedient to the authoritative figure. In the same way, demons and infirmities of the body are quite different yet still both are under the authority that was given to Jesus Christ by the Father through the Holy Spirit. Therefore both must come under subjection to that authority. In each situation both demon and malady obeyed the authority of Christ and it resulted in the miracle of divine healing.

The Same Incident According To Matthew and Mark

---

[46] Chavda, Mahesh. THE HIDDEN POWER OF HEALING PRAYER. Destiny Image Publishers INC. 2001. Pg. 62

[88]

"And he touched her hand, and the fever left her: and she arose, and ministered unto them." (*Matthew 8: 15*)

Matthew says that Jesus only touched Simon's mother-in-law's hand and she was healed as was the case with most other individuals whom He ministered to. The people were healed because the Spirit of the Lord who administered the healing lived within Jesus' physical body and flowed into the recipient's body at the point of contact, where Jesus touched the person or where the person touched Jesus. According to Maldonado, Jesus healed the woman by impartation.[47]

"And he came and took her by the hand, and lifted her up; and immediately the fever left her, and she ministered unto them." (*Mark 1: 31*)

Mark records that Jesus not only commanded healing, but acted on His command by helping Simon's mother-in-law to get up to complete her healing.

According to Matthew, Mark and Luke Jesus did the following three actions in healing Peter's mother-in-law:

• He chided the fever.

• He made contact with her hand.

• He assisted her up from her bed.

---

[47] Maldonado, Guillermo. Jesus Heals your sickness today. ERJ Publications.2009. Pg. 114

- There was no intercession made for her.

Only if a follower of Christ, believes the words that are found in John 14:12 are true can he/she be as effective as Jesus was in the administration of healing of Simon's mother-in-law.

"Verily, verily, I say unto you, He that believeth on me, the works that I do shall he do also; and greater works than these shall he do; because I go unto my Father." (John 14:12)

It is important to rise up to the challenge in order to do the same thing that Jesus did in healing Peter's mother in law. It is important to understand that visible results were part of Jesus' ministry on the earth. It is important to learn exactly how Jesus rebuked the infirmity. The correct approach to rebuking sicknesses or demons is of the utmost importance. If you fail to follow the commanding procedure that Jesus has laid out in the Scriptures the results would be an unhealed individual.[48]

Jesus Used Authority and the Laying On Of Hands to Heal

"When the sun was setting, the people brought to Jesus all who had various kinds of sickness, and laying his hands on each one, he healed them.

---

[48] Maldonado, Guillermo. Jesus Heals your sickness today. ERJ Publications.2009. Pg. 127

Moreover, demons came out of many people, shouting, "You are the Son of God!" But he rebuked them and would not allow them to speak, because they knew he was the Christ." (Luke 4: 40-41)

In administering divine healing to the people, Jesus employed two principles that He has repeated throughout His ministry, they are as follows: First, the laying on of hands, where Jesus made physical contact with the possessed individual or infirmed individual to the Holy Spirit residing within Him. Secondly, the use of authoritative commands directed to either an evil spirit or physical abnormality in an individual. [49]

A Man with Leprosy

"While Jesus was in a certain city, a man came along who was covered with leprosy. When he saw Jesus, he fell with his face to the ground and begged him, 'Lord, if you are willing, you can make me clean.' Jesus reached out his hand and touched the man saying, 'I am willing, be clean!' And immediately the leprosy left him." (Luke 5: 12, 13)

---

[49] Maldonado, Guillermo. Jesus Heals your sickness today. ERJ Publications.2009. Pg. 113

Here we see the gentleman in question was not demon possessed but rather he suffered from a medical condition that was identified as leprosy.[50]

   As was His practice, Jesus laid His hand upon His leprous patient and the leprosy left the patient's body.

Did Jesus intercede for this man? There's no biblical evidence to suggest that Jesus interceded on the leper's behalf to His Heavenly Father for the healing the leper received.

Did Jesus say: "Father, we command this man to be clean?" According to the Scriptures, Jesus only commanded the sickness to be gone. Again, there was no intercession made to the Father which is a common misconception many Christians make in the process of administering healing to others.

• Did Jesus close his eyes? No, there is no biblical evidence to support that claim. Many believers today close their eyes when they are ministering to the sick and or demon possessed.

• Was there any priestly component such as petitions or blessings to the Father? No, the action was absolutely kingly in nature, a direct authoritative command to a medical condition.

---

[50]   WebMD.   Leprosy   Overview.   WebMD.< http://www.webmd.com/skin-problems-and-treatments/guide/leprosy-symptoms-treatments-history> Retrieved on 3/31/14

This miracle was brought about in two parts. First, there was the formation of a connection between the Holy Spirit to the infirmed individual by the laying on of Jesus' hands, the impartation, and second, by executing the authority that Jesus had over physical abnormalities of the body. Jesus spoke the command and the body responded in normalizing itself, resulting in the infirmity leaving the body. [51] [52]

Mountain-Moving Faith

In exorcising a demon or healing an infirmed individual, a believer must possess the authority that is given to them by the Holy Spirit. However, there is an additional feature that is also needed. It is called "mountain-moving faith." Mountain-moving faith parallels authority resulting in a demon being cast out or an infirm person being healed. Therefore, let us focus on this important variable known as "mountain-moving faith." Exactly what is mountain-moving faith?

Mountain-moving faith "means to believe God's Word the same way God believes it." [53]

" And on the morrow, when they were come from Bethany, he was hungry: And seeing a fig tree afar off having leaves, he came, if haply he might

---

[51] Maldonado, Guillermo. Jesus Heals your sickness today. ERJ Publications.2009. Pg. 114
[52] Trimm, Cindy. Commanding Your Morning. Charisma House. 2007 Pg. 113
[53] Maldonado, Guillermo. Jesus Heals your sickness today. ERJ Publications.2009. Pg. 106

find anything thereon: and when he came to it, he found nothing but leaves; for the time of figs was not yet. And Jesus answered and said unto it, No man eat fruit of thee hereafter forever. And his disciples heard it." (Mark 11: 12-14)

Jesus Talks To a Tree

Jesus spoke to the fig tree, cursed it in the presence of His disciples, and then commanded the tree to die because it was not producing fruit. Jesus knew He had authority over the tree but not only did He know He had the authority, He "believed" He had the authority and His belief and faith executed the authority He had over the tree. There was no need to ask the Father's permission to curse the tree because the authority was already given and executed by faith. What was the immediate result of Jesus speaking to the fig tree?

The fig tree withered, it heard and obeyed the words that Jesus spoke over it.

"In the morning, as they went along, they saw the fig tree withered from the roots. Peter remembered and said to Jesus, Rabbi, look! The fig tree you cursed has withered!" (Mark 11: 20, 21)

Peter was astonished. Of the twelve disciples, Peter always had a special interest in the miracles that Jesus performed. In Matthew 14, when the twelve disciples saw Jesus walking on the water, Peter was the only one who put his faith into action and asked to perform the same miracle to walk on the water as Jesus did.

Remembering how Jesus cursed the fig tree and it obeyed and seeing Jesus walking on the water, Peter was intrigued and wanted to understand how Jesus performed both miracles. How did Jesus use his authority to curse the fig tree? His reply in the next verse reveals the answer.

"Have faith of God," Jesus answered (Mark 11: 22).

Another English translation, Young's Literal Translation, according to the original Greek transcript the word "in" is replaced with the word "of".[54] [55] This is significant, since there is a clear distinction where Jesus is saying not only to have faith in God but also have faith like God. Here Jesus was explaining to Peter how he performed the miracles. It was done not only by the authority He received from the Holy Spirit but also by His faith of God and His faith in the authority that He received. [56] The answer of having faith in God is very vague and does not give a descriptive physical explanation of the miracle. However, "Faith of God" offers

---

[54] Mark: Chapter 11, Verse 22 THE HOLY BIBLE. (King James Version) Brown and Marley.
[55] Mark: Chapter 11, Verse 22 THE HOLY BIBLE. (Young's Literal Translation). Robert Young
[56] THE NEW PROOF PRODUCERS / Dr. Morris Cerullo – Pg 125, quoted with permission. Copyright 1998-2014 Morris Cerullo World Evangelism. All Rights Reserved. www.mcwe.com

a general understanding of how the miracle was performed.[57]

Faith of God

In the next verse, Jesus goes on to explain the nature of "faith of God."

"I tell you the truth, if anyone says to this mountain, 'Go, throw yourself into the sea.'" (Mark 11: 23)

The above verse talks about what Jesus said when His disciples approached Him after failing to deliver a boy from epilepsy. In essence, Jesus replied to them that they failed because of their little faith. Here Jesus wasn't talking about faith as a mustard seed; He was talking about mountain-moving faith. Jesus then specifies the nature of mountain-moving faith.[58]

"And does not doubt in his heart but believes that what he says will happen, it will be done for him." (Mark 11: 24)

Faith of God therefore consists of two ingredients:

- No doubt

[57] THE NEW PROOF PRODUCERS / Dr. Morris Cerullo – Pg 126, quoted with permission. Copyright 1998-2014 Morris Cerullo World Evangelism. All Rights Reserved. www.mcwe.com
[58] Demolishing Demonic Strongholds / Dr. Morris Cerullo — Pg. 203, quoted with permission. Copyright 2012-2014 MORRIS CERULLO WORLD EVANGELISM. All Rights Reserved. www.mcwe.com

- Believing our spoken words will come to pass

Four Illustrations of "Faith of God"

To get a clear picture of what the faith of God entails, we will look at four illustrations.

How Would God Move A Mountain Apart From The Hand Of Man?

From the beginning God has spoken things into being. He did not pray because there is no one higher than him to pray to. So, He speaks a command and the spiritual and physical realms obey Him.

> *"And answering Jesus said to them, Have faith of God. For truly I say to you that whoever shall say to this mountain, Be moved and be cast into the sea..." (Mark 11: 22-23).*

When God issues a command, He expects it to be done. Does He have any doubt that the mountain will obey Him? Is He fearful that the mountain may not move? Does He believe that the mountain will not obey Him? The answers are all no; there is absolutely no doubt, disbelief, or fear that His commands will not be obeyed.

There is no doubt because God knows that He has authority over the mountain, it will of course obey His commands. Therefore when God speaks with mountain-moving faith, or faith of God, the mountain obeys His command. Faith of God is related to authority and vice versa. Believers must now issue their commands with no doubt or fear that their commands will be obeyed. That is having the faith of God.

Illustration One: "Let There Be Light"

In the beginning God created the heavens and the earth. And God said, "Let there be light." God essentially spoke the light into existence. Let us assume that there were angels present at that point. When God spoke, "Let there be light," did He harbour any doubt at all that the light would in fact obey His command and appear? Was He concerned that if the light did not appear, He might be embarrassed in front of the angels? No, God had no doubt at all. Why not?

God had no doubt the light would appear because He knew He had supreme authority over the light, and that it would obey His command. Therefore when He said, "Let there be light," He spoke it forth with the mountain-moving faith that He possessed. The knowledge and understanding of authority over something rises to the level of faith of God and enables believers to command with total confidence.[59]

Illustration Two: Jesus Raising Lazarus from The Dead

[59] THE NEW PROOF PRODUCERS / Dr. Morris Cerullo – Pg 308-309, quoted with permission. Copyright 1998-2014 Morris Cerullo World Evangelism. All Rights Reserved. www.mcwe.com

When Jesus stood before the tomb containing the corpse of Lazarus, He was accompanied by the sisters of Lazarus, Mary and Martha, as well as some Jews. (John 11) Jesus spoke forth the command, saying, "Lazarus, come out!" When Jesus did so, it was with all power and authority that He knew he possessed. Was it possible that He could have had doubt that the dead man would come back to life? Was He afraid that if this miracle did not happen, Mary and Martha would no longer believe in Him and He would be ostracized by the Jews? No, there was no doubt. Why not?

Jesus knew that the Father had given Him authority to raise the dead. (John 5: 21) Because of this authority Jesus commanded Lazarus with faith of God. If you know that you have been given authority over something, you can issue a command with faith of God and with great confidence without wavering and it shall be done.[60]

Illustration Three: Telling Your Dog to 'Sit'

You have had one dog since he was a puppy and named him Blackie, and countless dollars were spent sending him to obedience school. You have some friends over one day and you decide that you want to show your friends how obedient your dog Blackie is. Blackie comes in the room, you command him to come to you, he does, you

---

[60] THE NEW PROOF PRODUCERS / Dr. Morris Cerullo – Pg 308-309, quoted with permission. Copyright 1998-2014 Morris Cerullo World Evangelism. All Rights Reserved. www.mcwe.com

command him to sit, he does, you command him to lie down and he does. Do you doubt that Blackie will obey all your commands in front of your friends? Do you fear that Blackie will disobey your command and ruin your illustration, and embarrass you in front of your friends? Of course not! Why not?

You knew that Blackie would obey every command you gave him because you trusted in the fact that he had been to obedience school and was properly trained. You also know that you are the master and he is the subject, you have authority over him and you have trained him to yield to that authority. You have no doubt that Blackie will sit and that he will in fact do what you say because you know that you have authority over him.

With this authority you can issue a command to him with faith of God and no doubt, with complete confidence and assurance and without any wavering. What if Blackie is stubborn and doesn't sit? Will you prostrate yourself onto the floor and cry out to Jesus to help you? No, you will simply repeat the command with even greater force and authority and may even reach out your hand to force him to sit. One way or another, he is going to submit to your command.

Here is an illustration of issuing the command to your dog without faith of God. It's exaggerated and dramatized, but you will get the point.

Blackie is standing before you. He is awaiting your authoritative command. But you lie on the floor before him, and gently say, "Good dog, Blackie. I love you, and Jesus loves you too." You plead with him, "Would you please sit, Blackie?" Then you look up to heaven. "Jesus, help me! I can do nothing, this is impossible for me, but nothing is impossible for you. Please make Blackie sit, thank you Jesus, thank you Father." You follow with unknown tongues. Then you turn back to Blackie and say, "Blessed dog, Blackie, if you don't mind, would you please sit?"

In using this method, Blackie is not going to be obedient, it is not enough to know you have the authority over him; it is the way in which you present yourself, it is the way in which you issue the command, your body language, your tone of voice, your posture. As a result, nothing happens. Blackie just wags his tail and licks your face.

Unfortunately, many believers attempt to heal the sick and cast out evil spirits this way. They do not understand how to give commands with faith of God; instead they interchange praying and commanding. They cry out to Jesus and give thanks to God thinking this makes Him act. Charismatic believers may in addition speak in unknown tongues for prolonged periods of time. [61] It is clear that such believers are not properly trained and that

---

[61] THE NEW PROOF PRODUCERS / Dr. Morris Cerullo – Pg 26, quoted with permission. Copyright 1998-2014 Morris Cerullo World Evangelism. All Rights Reserved. www.mcwe.com

they have doubt. It is not surprising why the infirmity or demon does not obey them, and they fail.

Illustration Four: Correction of a Child

Similarly, when commanding your five-year old son to stop hitting his little brother, you are not on your knees pleading with your five year old, your tone of voice is not sweet and gentle and you certainly do not cry to Jesus for help or speak in tongues. You stand upright with your eyes focused, facial expression serious and your voice stern. The commands of your mouth should be quick and sharp; there is no room for "ifs" or "buts." Your five-year-old knows that you mean business and knows that if he does not obey there will be consequences. There is no room for doubt or questioning in your mind that this child will be punished if he does not obey. You must approach your administration of healing or exorcising of demons in like manner with no fear, no doubt, just absolute faith.[62]

Authority and Mountain-Moving Faith

The Greek word for authority is "exousia,"[63] it can be compared to "potential energy" in a believer given by

---

[62] THE NEW PROOF PRODUCERS / Dr. Morris Cerullo – Pg 229, quoted with permission. Copyright 1998-2014 Morris Cerullo World Evangelism. All Rights Reserved. www.mcwe.com

[63] Thayer, Joseph H. Thayer's Greek-English Lexicon of the New Testament. Hendrickson Publishers. 2007. Pg.225

Jesus to heal the sick: but authority by itself is insufficient. How can this authority be changed into an actual physical force of healing in evangelism? That is where mountain-moving faith comes in or having faith like God. Giving an order with mountain-moving faith transforms the "potential energy" into an actual physical force of healing.

In some charismatic and Pentecostal churches, there is an emphasis on seeking "the anointing."[64] It is taught that with "the anointing" disciples shall be able to create miraculous signs to edify God. The New Testament has never mentioned "the anointing" on a follower of Jesus Christ which empowers that individual to heal the sick, cast out demons, or to minister to others through the power of the Holy Spirit. In the situation with the epileptic boy Jesus specifically meant "faith of God." If you go back to the basics of the Scriptures, you will see that it is not the lack of an anointing or authority that prevents healing but rather a lack of mountain moving faith on the disciple's part.

Authority versus the Gift of Healing

The use of authority follows the kingly office. As stated in the book of Acts, the disciples followed the same principles when using their authority to heal. The gift of healing operates completely different as opposed to healing

---

[64] Chavda, Mahesh. The Hidden Power Healing Prayer. Destiny Image Publishers, Inc. 2001. Pg. 1-15

with authority.[65] [66] With the gift of healing, prayer may be involved in different forms followed by a priestly component involving some edification of God and thanksgiving. Pentecostals may even pray in other tongues when ministering with the gift of healing. [67]

The Importance of Prayer and Fasting

"But this kind does not go out except by prayer and fasting." (Matthew 17: 21)

Some believers may think that Jesus is saying that some demons are subjected by authority and commands, but some are subjected to prayer and fasting. This is not what Jesus meant, the disciples failed to cast out demons because they lacked sufficient mountain-moving faith. Jesus' remedy for increasing their mountain-moving faith was prayer and fasting. According to Charles R Thomas, "There is unlimited and untapped power available to you through effective prayer and fasting."[68] By increasing one's mounting-moving faith by prayer and fasting then all

---

[65] Nineteen Gifts of God to His Children, by Dr. Terrence Jenkins, p.78-81. Copyright 1991, 48 HrBooks. Used by permission

[66] Chavda, Mahesh. The Hidden Power Healing Prayer. Destiny Image Publishers, Inc. 2001. Pg. 51-63

[67] THE NEW PROOF PRODUCERS / Dr. Morris Cerullo – Pg 26, quoted with permission. Copyright 1998-2014 Morris Cerullo World Evangelism. All Rights Reserved. www.mcwe.com

[68] Thomas, Charles R. LIVING in GOD'S KINGDOM on EARTH. Xulon Press. 2007. Pg. 63

demonic entities as well as infirmities will obey each and every command the disciple speaks.[69]

Jesus Does Distance Healing

Jesus was original; He was an innovator, not bound by tradition and ritualistic laws. He was not set in His ways; every situation He encountered was approached from a different perspective and procedure. The method to this "madness" is that every situation is unique, and a procedure that will work for one healing may not work for another. At one time He would lay His hands, or just speak a command without laying hands. One time He spat on the ground, made clay and put it on the person's eye. Sometimes a person only needed to touch the hem of His garment. Then there were those times where Jesus would speak the word only and the person who was a great distance away would be healed.

Healing The Centurion's Servant

The story of the healing of the centurion's servant is found in Luke 7:1-10. Distance healing is based solely on exercising the authority that was given to Jesus by God the Father through the Holy Spirit. The centurion's initial desire was for Jesus to accompany him to his house and

---

[69] Demolishing Demonic Strongholds / Dr. Morris Cerullo — Pg 221-230, quoted with permission.

heal his sick servant by physical contact.[70] John G Lake says, "So a person who is not even a Christian can have faith for someone else."[71] However, he realized that Jesus walked in authority. Being a man of authority in the physical realm, he submitted to his superiors and the soldiers of lesser rank, submitted to him without question. He knew the chain of command inside and out so he understood that physical contact was not necessary to execute a command and thus requested Jesus to only speak the command in complete faith and it would be executed because of the authority that Jesus possessed "God's Rhema Word."[72] The centurion understood that the authoritative command issued by Jesus is comparable to a modern day nuclear missile that when launched/spoken in the spiritual realm has the ability to annihilate every infirmity, disease and demonic entity on the planet/physical realm.

Authority in the Natural Parallels Authority in the Spirit

Being of a military background, the centurion understood the power of the chain of command and realized that just as authority is in the natural, it is the same

---

[70] THE NEW PROOF PRODUCERS / Dr. Morris Cerullo – Pg. 209-210, quoted with permission. Copyright 1998-2014 Morris Cerullo World Evangelism. All Rights Reserved. www.mcwe.com
[71] Lake, John G. Divine Healing Technician Training Manual. John G Lake Ministries. 2006. Pg. 38
[72] Maldonado, Guillermo. Jesus Heals your sickness today. ERJ Publications.2009. Pg. 116

in the spiritual realm.[73] When the centurion is given an order from his superiors, he obeys without question and when he issues orders to his soldiers they obey without question. So naturally, he concluded that when Jesus issued a command, all of heaven is subjected to that command and obeys without question. Similarly everything on earth and under the earth is subjected to His authority and must obey without question.

The centurion understood that authority is not affected by distance in the military so naturally it would not be affected in the spiritual realm. Orders are given to battleships on the other side of the earth from the command base via satellites, and the battleships execute the command even though they are on the other side of the planet. The bottom line is that Jesus had the authority over infirmities and demonic entities. If He issues a command, regardless of distance they must obey because they are subjected to His authority.

Jesus marvelled at the centurion's faith because this was a person who completely understood what He was talking about concerning authority. Even Jesus' disciples failed to grasp the full extent of what it meant to have complete authority and dominion over sicknesses, diseases, infirmities and demonic entities.

---

[73] THE NEW PROOF PRODUCERS / Dr. Morris Cerullo – Pg. 33-41, quoted with permission. Copyright 1998-2014 Morris Cerullo World Evangelism. All Rights Reserved. www.mcwe.com

The Ten Lepers

In Luke 17:11-19 Jesus healed the ten lepers. It is important to note, that there is not a limit in the number of people that can be healed at one time. We see this happened when Jesus healed ten lepers at one time. When the authoritative command of healing is given it does not matter if it is given to one person, ten people or a crowd of one million.[74] Jesus clearly said that believers would do greater things than He did. What did He mean by this? With the advancement in technology, believers are able to minister to hundreds of thousands and even millions of people around the globe at one time, through the Radio, the Television or the Internet. If a person truly understands the authority he/ she has been given by Jesus Christ and can effectively execute that authority, then there is no reason that one hundred thousand or even millions of people cannot be healed at one time.

Technological sources used in the 21st century to deliver ministry to the global community are as follows: Google Wave, YouTube/video, e mail, instant message, blogs, podcasting, forums, mailing lists, tumblogs, images (Flicker etc.), web-fax, social bookmarking, newsgroups, aggregation sites (HN/Metafilter/etc.), standard websites TV and movies.

---

[74] Wigglesworth, Smith. Smith Wigglesworth on Healing. Whitaker House. 1999. Pg 116-117

Older forms still in use to minister healing at a distance are: letters, phone, mail, fax, books, magazines, pamphlets, essays, poetry, speech, sign language, textbooks, meetings, signs, paintings, music, radio, notes, memos, speeches and lectures.

Chapter Seven

Why Did Jesus Heal?

Jesus healed the ailing people with three basic agendas:

1. To show to the unbelievers that Jesus Christ is the Son of God and the Saviour of the world. [75]
2. Jesus worked via the Law of Redemption, this was evident because of the abundance of compassion Jesus had toward suffering humanity. [76]
3. Simply as a visual aid in teaching his disciples how to heal. [77]

The task is to follow the exact pattern set out by Jesus Christ and his early disciples. Christ came to save the lost. The miracles that He performed were for the primary purpose of convincing the lost to believe in Him as their Messiah. The purpose of Jesus and His early disciples at that time remains the same to the believers' purpose even today. Therefore, it is of extreme importance to learn how

---

[75] Victory Miracle Library / Dr. Morris Cerullo – Pg. 1-6, quoted with permission. Copyright 1986-2014 Morris Cerullo World Evangelism. All Rights Reserved. www.mcwe.com

[76] Woodwood-Etter, Maria. Signs, and Wonders. Whitaker House.1997. Pg. 186

[77] THE NEW PROOF PRODUCERS / Dr. Morris Cerullo – Pg. 187-197, quoted with permission. Copyright 1998-2014 Morris Cerullo World Evangelism. All Rights Reserved. www.mcwe.com

Jesus went about ministering healing to the sick according to the gospels.

Any Believer Can Do This!

John 14: 12 *"Verily, verily, I say unto you, He that believeth on me, the works that I do shall he do also; and greater works than these shall he do; because I go unto my Father."*

The question arises "What did Jesus accomplish while here on earth?"

He taught about the kingdom of God, demonstrated the power of God by healing the afflicted, casting out demons and giving discipleship to those who were divinely chosen. The Word communicates that anyone believing in Jesus will do greater works in His name. Therefore it is important to carefully examine how the Lord healed the sick after being anointed by the Holy Ghost. In the same way believers follow Jesus' instructions to administer healing to the diseased.

"The Spirit of the Lord GOD is upon me; because the LORD hath anointed me to preach good tidings unto the meek; he hath sent me to bind up the broken hearted, to proclaim liberty to the captives..." (Isaiah 61: 1)

The prophet Isaiah foretold that God would consecrate the Messiah with the Spirit to accomplish His divine destiny.

This was achieved when Jesus was baptized in the River Jordan.

"Now when all the people were baptized, it came to pass, that Jesus also being baptized, and praying, the heaven was opened, And the Holy Ghost descended in a bodily shape like a dove upon him, and a voice came from heaven, which said, Thou art my beloved Son; in thee I am well pleased." (*Luke 3: 21, 22*)

"And Jesus being full of the Holy Ghost returned from Jordan, and was led by the Spirit into the wilderness, being forty days tempted of the devil. And in those days he did eat nothing: and when they were ended, he afterward hungered." (*Luke 4: 1, 2*)

After Jesus was filled with the Holy Spirit, he was led into the wilderness to fast and pray, over a forty day span, where he was also tempted by Satan. Jesus fasted prior to healing the sick and expelling demons to proclaim to the Israelites that he was the Messiah. Fasting is an essential element to a believer who desires to minister in authority and courage as Jesus did.

Chapter Eight

Correct Protocol in Healing

The Scripture is clear that there is more than one way to minister to the sick. For example, anointed oil and other items such as cloths and laying on of hands. Which method or approach an individual chooses can be related to the task or context in which the believer is involved. [78]

According to the Scripture, the gift of healing is primarily for ministering to sick believers. As such, the gift can manifest when believers congregate. Some churches may utilize a "Healing Room", where trained Christians minister to those who come for healing. Although Healing Rooms can be used by anyone who is not from the church community, they are most frequented by church members and fellow Christians. The miraculous healing manifestations which occur in a Healing Room may be the result of the gift of healing. [79]

Faith of God and Faith in God

There is a definite distinction between faith of God or mountain-moving faith that is moving in the kingly dimension or downward moving commands or orders

---

[78] THE NEW PROOF PRODUCERS / Dr. Morris Cerullo – Pg. 208-209, quoted with permission. Copyright 1998-2014 Morris Cerullo World Evangelism. All Rights Reserved. www.mcwe.com
[79] Blake, Curry. Divine Healing Technician Training Manual. www.jglm.org. 2006. Pg. 92

directed to demons, illnesses and other infirmities. Faith in God is in the priestly dimension of upward prayer, supplication, praise, worship and thanksgiving unto God. [80]

"...if anyone says to this mountain, 'Go, throw yourself into the sea,' and does not doubt in his heart but believes that what he says will happen, it will be done for him." (Mark 11: 23)

When we give a command to a mountain with no doubt in our heart, we are exercising faith of God.

"Therefore I tell you, whatever you ask for in prayer, believe that you have received it, and it will be yours." (Mark 11: 24)

The nature of our relationship with God is that of absolute trust, as verse 24 above teaches.

Next is the prophetic office (horizontal relationship) that believers operate in and it concerns the relationship the believers have with other believers and nonbelievers. The next verse from Mark 11 describes the nature of this relationship:

"And when ye stand praying, forgive, if ye have ought against any: that your Father also which is in

[80] THE NEW PROOF PRODUCERS / Dr. Morris Cerullo – Pg 137-154, quoted with permission. Copyright 1998-2014 Morris Cerullo World Evangelism. All Rights Reserved. www.mcwe.com

*heaven may forgive you your trespasses."(*Mark 11: 25)

The Lord teaches us to forgive others in order to receive forgiveness for ourselves.

The priestly, kingly and the prophetic realms are all intertwined. Having a strong relationship with God, an effective prayer life as well as fasting in the priestly realm, boosts mountain-moving faith in the kingly realm, which brings about healing and deliverance from infirmities and demonic entities. Forgiving others in the horizontal direction helps in both the priestly and kingly realms in that God will forgive you. [81] [82]

Activation of Faith of God

You will now apply what you have learned thus far. Be practical, have someone with you who needs healing so that you can actually practice what you have learned. Follow Jesus' actions; lay your hands on the person and command in the name of Jesus, healing to come forth. Limit your spoken commands according to the structure found in the Word of God. It is best not to go beyond what is written. [83]

---

[81] Maldonado, Guillermo. Jesus Heals your sickness today. ERJ Publications. 2009. Pg. 208-210

[82] Maldonado, Guillermo. Jesus Heals your sickness today. ERJ Publications.2009. Pg. 188-189

[83] Maldonado, Guillermo. Jesus Heals your sickness today. ERJ Publications.2009. Pg. 218

There are many examples of miraculous healing and deliverance that were performed by Jesus and the disciples in the Gospels as well as in the book of Acts. You can follow their example. Refer to chapter 10 and 11.

Now is the time to put into practice what you have learned thus far. It is advisable that you find someone who has a "small mountain" for your first time. From my experience it has been discovered that knee pains and back pains are small mountains and not difficult to drive out. Before you minister healing, this is when you take care of your "priestly" concerns and cleanse yourself before the Lord by praying to God, acknowledging that you forgive others and asking forgiveness for yourself. You can also ask God to use you to heal the infirmity and thank him for giving you the opportunity to do so.

At this point, you're stepping out of the priestly realm and into the kingly realm. From here onwards there will be no prayer to God. It is now the time for action with the use of authority, mountain-moving faith and supreme commands. Although scriptures do not speak of anyone ministering healing to himself, the principle of authority and the laying on of hands hold regardless of whether the pain is in someone else's body or in yours. [84]

---

[84] Chavda, Mahesh. The Hidden Power Healing Prayer. Destiny Image Publishers, Inc. 2001. Pg. 115-119

The Laying On Of Hands and the Exercise of Authority

As you lay your hand on the body, speak forth commands along the lines of the following:

"Pain, I rebuke you. Leave now in the Name of Jesus!"

"In the name of Jesus Christ, be healed!"

"Be restored in the name of Jesus!"

"Infirmity, leave now in the name of Jesus!"

"Be set free in the name of Jesus Christ!"

"Get up and walk in the name of Jesus!"[85] [86]

Issue the commands with no doubt or hesitation; speak directly and personally to the infirmity in the person. Speak sternly, harshly and even raise your voice at the pain. This is what *rebuking* entails. The pain is an "enemy" and we fight our enemies with violence. It will not leave willingly; it must be *forced out* with authority and faith of God. Expect the pain to hear your words and obey your commands. (Matthew 11: 12)

---

[85] THE NEW PROOF PRODUCERS / Dr. Morris Cerullo – Pg 216-219, quoted with permission. Copyright 1998-2014 Morris Cerullo World Evangelism. All Rights Reserved. www.mcwe.com
[86] Lord Teach us to Pray/ Dr. Morris Cerullo – Pg. 208 – 209, quoted with permission. Copyright 2004-2014 Morris Cerullo World Evangelism. All Rights Reserved www.mcwe.com

Ask the person if there is any change. Test the problematic area to see any manifested result. Jesus asked how people felt after the commanded healing. If the pain has dissipated, you have succeeded in moving the "mountain" into the sea.

If the pain is decreasing but not yet gone, it means that it is beginning to obey your orders. In this case, continue commanding the pain to leave in Jesus' name and continue asking the person how they are feeling, continue to do so until they report that the pain is completely gone.

If there are no changes from the first command, this is the point where doubt may set in. It is a test; you must press on and continue in faith. With each resistance of the pain, repeat the commands each time gaining in force and harshness and do not accept defeat. Continue rebuking the pain and eventually it will know that you are not giving up or backing down, it will know it must leave because there is no other option.[87]

Decorum for the Laying On Of Hands

Throughout His ministry Jesus placed His hands on infirm individuals and administered divine healing onto them. This is a crucial process of divine healing as it creates a physical point of contact, which allows the Spirit of God residing in Jesus Christ to flow into the afflicted.

---

[87] Chavda, Mahesh. The Hidden Power Healing Prayer. Destiny Image Publishers, Inc. 2001.Pg. 125-134

The Holy Spirit, which resided in Jesus Christ radiated so powerfully, even his garments served as a point of contact where healing could flow through. We see evidence of this where a woman was healed by simply touching his garment. (Mark 5: 24 -30) When Jesus touched the infirmed, healing flowed into them. [88]

Why Do Believers Lay Hands On The Sick?

"...Christ in you, the hope of glory."(Col. 1: 27)

"The laying of hands is one way God uses to transfer divine virtue, blessings, authority, power, wisdom, healing, and deliverance to us." Maldonado.[89]

The Holy Spirit dwells in each and every born again believer. It is the same Holy Spirit that dwelt in Jesus Christ. So, if a believer lays his or her hand on an ill person and commands the sickness to leave in Jesus' name then that person is healed by the healing power of the Holy Spirit which flows from the believer into the sick person through the authority as power of attorney given to the believer by Jesus Christ over infirmities and demons.

When the woman had touched his garment, Jesus acknowledged there was a release of power. He felt it, and as a result searched to find out who had touched him with

---

[88] Maldonado, Guillermo. Jesus heals your sickness today. ERJ Publications.2009.Pg. 119

[89] Maldonado, Guillermo. Jesus Heals your sickness today. ERJ Publications. 2009. Pg. 113

faith and expectancy. (Mark 5: 30) Likewise, believers may sense a power outflow of healing at work when they lay hands on the ill or demon possessed. This is the law of impartation. There is a release from the believer and the recipient receives what is being imparted into his/her spirit.[90]

Where Should Believers Lay Hands On The Sick?

To achieve success in the art of laying hands on the sick, it is imperative to follow the outline of the procedures in the Gospels. It must be noted that Jesus never laid his hands inappropriately on any individual. Therefore we should follow likewise. If any individual has a pain from below the shoulder level, ask the individual to place his or her own hands on the affected area and issue the authoritative command. Do not rub, massage, squeeze, or slap the affected part of the person's body. Jesus did not do these things and such should be avoided.[91]

In administering healing to a deaf and mute man, Jesus placed his finger directly in the man's ear. Jesus knew that he must place his hands directly on or over the affected area. In this manner, Jesus was specific in his

---

[90] Maldonado, Guillermo. Jesus Heals your sickness today. ERJ Publications. 2009. Pg. 113-114

[91] Victory Miracle Library / Dr. Morris Cerullo – Pg 2, quoted with permission. Copyright 1986 -2014 Morris Cerullo World Evangelism. All Rights Reserved. www.mcwe.com

administration of healing. He was not interested in a long and drawn out process.

> *"Then he spit and touched the man's tongue and the Lord looked up to heaven and with a deep sigh said to him, "Ephphatha!" which means, "Be opened!""* (Mark 7: 33-34)

Jesus laid the axe directly to the root of the above physical infirmity. Jesus touched the man's tongue so that the healing power that resided in him would flow directly and proficiently unto the man's tongue and nowhere else. Jesus also spoke to the man's ears and demanded them to "be opened." Two actions are being achieved, the laying on of hands and the implementation of authority by releasing a command. Jesus never physically manipulated any part of the body when He healed the infirm. Therefore, believers should generally avoid such actions when healing the sick, as these practices are not scriptural.

> *"At this, the man's ears were opened, his tongue was loosened and he began to speak plainly."* *(Mark 7: 35)*

Believers must emulate the same pattern as Jesus did when ministering to those with hearing (and/or speech) problems. If they are wearing any technological aids, they should be removed. You must implant your fingers all the way into the ears. Command their ears to be opened in Jesus' name. It may not always be a physical infirmity; in some cases a spirit that needs to be cast out in Jesus' name may cause the loss of hearing. The individual's hearing must be checked after the command was issued and repeated until full restoration of hearing is achieved.

Where Did Jesus Place His Hands To Heal The Blind?

"A blind man was brought to Jesus and begged Jesus to touch him. Jesus pulled him aside and spit on his eyes and asked him if he saw anything." (Mark 8: 22-23)

Practicing accuracy and precision, Jesus spat directly into the man's eyes and placed His hands directly on the blind man eyes. Jesus asked the man, "Do you see anything?"

Jesus did not doubt when He asked because He expected something to occur. Jesus knew the infirmity was under His authority and He expected it to surrender to Him. If you truly understand the authority that was given to you by Jesus Christ, there should be no fear in asking the infirmed individual to confirm any changes that was made to them by healing when the authoritative command was given and hands were laid upon them.

"He looked up and said, "I see people; they look like trees walking around." (Mark 8: 24)

The man was only somewhat healed of his handicap of the eyes. Jesus laid hands again.

"Once more Jesus put his hands on the man's eyes. Then his eyes were opened, his sight was restored, and he saw everything clearly." (Mark 8: 25)

Even though you follow the protocol laid out by Jesus regarding healing, just as it happened to Jesus where He laid His hand on the blind man more than once, so to you may have to repeat the authoritative command and lay your hands on the infirm repeatedly, to achieve complete healing.

It is possible that un-confessed sins can hinder healing according to:

"Confess your faults one to another, and pray one for another, that ye may be healed. The effectual fervent prayer of a righteous man availeth much." (James 5: 16) [92]

Jesus's Secret to the Success of His Ministry Was His Prayer Life

"Jesus would pray for five hours and later only need two seconds to heal the blind man. I want you to notice the following principle: Jesus spent hours doing one thing and seconds doing another. We do things the other way around: spend a few minutes with God and then take many hours ministering to the people in His name. Hours spent with God make

---

[92] Maldonado, Guillermo. How to Minister Deliverance. ERJ Publications. 2004.Pg 25

the time we spend with people more effective."
Guillermo Maldonado. [93]

In order to see effectiveness in our ministry to the sick, we must do as Jesus did, which was to spend quality time praying and in fellowship with God.[94]

[93] Maldonado, Guillermo. PRAYER. DISCOVER THE SECRET TO EFFECTIVE PRAYER. ERJ Publicaciones. 2006. Pg. 19
[94] Demolishing Demonic Strongholds / Dr. Morris Cerullo — Pg 198, quoted with permission. Copyright 2012-2014 MORRIS CERULLO WORLD EVANGELISM. All Rights Reserved. www.mcwe.com

Chapter Nine

Failure of Disciples

When a military officer commands someone who is under his authority, he commands with no doubt or fear of being disobeyed. Because he has been given authority in that realm, he believes that what he commands will be executed.[95]

Disciples of Jesus Christ who are sent out to proclaim the Kingdom of God have been given authority over diseases and demons. When in this evangelistic context believers command diseases and demons to go in Jesus' Name, they speak with faith of God, without doubt and fear of failure.[96]

Authority over sickness and devils must be used in conjunction with faith of God or mountain-moving faith. The result of the absence of faith of God would be failure.

Now we understand why the disciples failed to exorcise the evil spirit. According to Jesus, they did not possess mountain-moving faith when they met the demon;

---

[95] THE NEW PROOF PRODUCERS / Dr. Morris Cerullo – Pg. 209, quoted with permission. Copyright 1998-2014 Morris Cerullo World Evangelism. All Rights Reserved. www.mcwe.com

[96] Lord Teach us to Pray/ Dr. Morris Cerullo – Pg. 209, quoted with permission. Copyright 2004-2014 Morris Cerullo World Evangelism. All Rights Reserved www.mcwe.com

in other words, they lacked faith of God. Demons that manifest as severe epilepsy can be intimidating and frightful to the inexperienced disciple. They can physically manipulate their victim, which results in uncontrollable convulsions. After hearing about the great power of the demon from the parent, there is a possibility that the disciples doubted their authority in their mind and so were reluctant to confront the demon and deliver the boy. However, after pleading requests from the parent they thought they would at least try.

When they stood by the boy and commanded the demon to leave, they did so without confidence, conviction and assurance. The demon sensed their lack of authority and power in the tone of their voice and realized that they had doubts about the authority and power they had. What was the result? *The demon refused to obey their commands to leave.*[97]

Here is an example of displaying doubt and lack of faith of God when trying to heal the sick or cast out a devil from an individual. You come close to the sick individual lacking confidence that anything will happen. You are hoping that Jesus will show up and a miracle will manifest. The individual needs a physical healing. You put your hands on the infirm person and close your eyes thinking that closing your eyes will manifest God's healing power.

---

[97] Maldonado, Guillermo. Jesus Heals your sickness today. ERJ Publications.2009. Pg. 94-109

You know that you really need God's help in order to heal the person, so you call upon His name: "Father, in the name of Jesus, let this infirmity leave!"

First error: If you want to minister to the sick, you should be addressing the infirmity and commanding it to go. Why are you speaking to the Father at all? Does it make any sense to tell the Father what you want the infirmity to do?[98]

Then you redirect your eyes back to God in heaven. And say to Him, "Thank you, God."

Second error: Why are you giving God glory when you should be addressing the infirmity and ordering it to leave in Jesus' name? It seems that you are trying to "bribe" God with thanks and good behavior; do you think you would get in his presence and receive the miracle? [99]

Then you redirect your attention to the infirmity, which should be under your authority. You force the words out through your lips, "I rebuke you in the name of Jesus Christ!" You can barely keep the quivering in your voice from manifesting. You are questioning yourself if anything is actually taking place, or if you are just making a clown

---

[98] THE NEW PROOF PRODUCERS / Dr. Morris Cerullo – Pg. 217, quoted with permission. Copyright 1998-2014 Morris Cerullo World Evangelism. All Rights Reserved. www.mcwe.com
[99] THE NEW PROOF PRODUCERS / Dr. Morris Cerullo – Pg. 230, quoted with permission. Copyright 1998-2014 Morris Cerullo World Evangelism. All Rights Reserved. www.mcwe.com

of yourself in front of the sick person and or the audience present.

Third error: The sound of your voice, your words and body language tell of the fear and doubt in your heart.[100]

You shout out, "Help me, Lord. I am helpless. But nothing is impossible for you. Please come to my aid." You then take a few seconds to magnify Him.

Fourth error: By requesting help from the Lord, you have revealed to everyone including the infirmity and or demon that you doubt your authority and so you need help from God in order to complete the healing and/or deliverance.[101]

About this time the charismatic or Pentecostal persuasion might be speaking in unknown tongues.

Fifth error: When believers speak in other tongues they are communicating with God (1 Corinthians 14: 2). Now is not the time to be communicating with God, now is the time to command the infirmity to leave. Would the

---

[100] Demolishing Demonic Strongholds / Dr. Morris Cerullo — Pg. 39-46, quoted with permission. Copyright 2012-2014 MORRIS CERULLO WORLD EVANGELISM. All Rights Reserved. www.mcwe.com

[101] Demolishing Demonic Strongholds / Dr. Morris Cerullo — Pg. 39-46, quoted with permission. Copyright 2012-2014 MORRIS CERULLO WORLD EVANGELISM. All Rights Reserved. www.mcwe.com

infirmity understand what you are saying when you speak in other tongues?

Charismatic believers have been trained that "when in doubt, speak in tongues." But what impression does this give to the demon or infirmity when you speak in tongues as you try to cast it out? The fear and doubt in your heart have been revealed through the words of your mouth. (Matthew 12: 34)[102]

Then you turn your focus to the afflicted person. "Abba, nothing is impossible for you. Be healed in the Name of Jesus!"

Sixth error: Why are you reminding Abba that nothing is impossible for Him? Of course He is able. God wants to use you to minister healing to the afflicted person. When you intertwine praying and commanding you are exposing the disbelief in your hearts to the afflicted person, the affliction, the evil spirits, and any other audience. You are making a statement saying that you do need help from the Father to perform this miracle. As a result the disease or demon will not succumb to your command.

Jesus never intertwined praying and commanding when He healed the sick neither did His apostles when they administered healing to the sick. Both Jesus and His

---

[102] THE NEW PROOF PRODUCERS / Dr. Morris Cerullo – Pg. 22-24, quoted with permission. Copyright 1998-2014 Morris Cerullo World Evangelism. All Rights Reserved. www.mcwe.com

apostles separated prayer time from miraculous works. Why is it so important to understand this concept?

Praying and commanding are activities of two different offices in the government of God. Praying belongs to the priestly office, while commanding is a part of the kingly office. As such both cannot operate at the same time. They both are going in different directions. The priestly actions are directed to God, and the kingly actions are directed down to things, which are under the believer's authority, therefore it is impossible to go in two different directions at the same time. It is also disrespectful to address God and demons at the same time. This is an unfortunate practice that most believers do today due to the fact that they have not been properly trained in proper spiritual protocol and as a result they fail to manifest healing as Jesus taught His early disciples. [103]

Lack of Mountain-Moving Faith

> *"And Jesus said unto them, Because of your unbelief: for verily I say unto you, If ye have faith as a grain of mustard seed, ye shall say unto this mountain, Remove hence to yonder place; and it shall remove; and nothing shall be impossible unto you."(Matthew 17: 20)*

---

[103] Maldonado, Guillermo. Jesus Heals your sickness today. ERJ Publications.2009. Pg. 94

According to Jesus, the disciples lacked faith of God or "mountain-moving faith." If they had this kind of faith, they could speak to any obstacle and order it to get out. The obstacle would then obey and the evil spirit would have listened to them and left the child and nothing would be impossible for them. Jesus had already dispensed divine authority upon his disciples. Authority by itself is insufficient. Authority must be paralleled with mountain-moving faith.

We will now address the nature of mountain-moving faith. Jesus revealed to them that their failure was due to small mountain-moving faith. They needed to acquire more of this faith. Jesus taught them a way in which they could elevate their mountain-moving faith.[104]

Why Do We Fail To Heal The Sick?

> *"And when they were come to the multitude, there came to him a certain man, kneeling down to him, and saying, Lord, have mercy on my son: for he is lunatick, and sore vexed: for ofttimes he falleth into the fire, and oft into the water. And I brought him to thy disciples, and they could not cure him."(Matthew 17: 14-16)*

---

[104] THE NEW PROOF PRODUCERS / Dr. Morris Cerullo – Pg. 137-147, quoted with permission. Copyright 1998-2014 Morris Cerullo World Evangelism. All Rights Reserved. www.mcwe.com

The boy suffered with severe epilepsy. His dad brought him to Jesus' disciples, but they could not heal him. They failed at attempting to cast out the demon and heal the boy of his suffering. Jesus' outlook after hearing the news about how his disciples botched the miracle was both amazing and revealing.

> Jesus responded by saying, *"O faithless and perverse generation, "how long shall I be with you? How long shall I suffer you?"* (Matthew 17:17)

> According to F.F. Bosworth, "Some are not healed because of unbelief on the part of the elder or minister who prays for them."[105]

Jesus was very disappointed with His disciples and He showed this by reproaching them. They could not understand why Jesus was disappointed. To them it was just one failed attempt of driving out a demon. Yet still Jesus was displeased.

> "We cannot receive the authority in the resurrection until we have been tested in the authority that comes through obedience; we must follow the same steps that Jesus had to follow. Many believers are unable to enjoy the authority in the resurrection because they never submit to their authority" [106]

---

[105] Bosworth, F.F. Christ T.H.E. Healer. Fleming H. Revell.1973. Pg. 182

[106] Maldonado, Guillermo. HOW TO MINISTER DELIVERENCE. ERJ Publications. 2004. Pg. 42

Guillermo Maldonado.

Many believers today are lukewarm, in that they are in God and in the world as well. In order to fully wield our God given authority, we must fully submit to obeying all that God demands of us.

Why Was Jesus Tired And Irritable?

After being on the mountain of transfiguration all day it can be suggested that Jesus was tired and hungry, so He reacted as any normal person would react when confronted in a similar situation. Could this possibly explain Jesus' reaction to the situation? The answer is no. Jesus expected His disciples to perform the miracle successfully. He had hoped that they would have understood their authority that He gave them.

How Could Jesus Have Possibly <u>Expected</u> His Disciples To Perform The Miracle?

There are three reasons:

• The disciples were in training under Jesus' command, they observed Him and learned from Him as He healed the sick and delivered the demon possessed.

• Jesus had bestowed upon His disciples the same authority that was given unto Him from the Holy Spirit.

- He specifically sent them out and commanded them to heal the sick and deliver the demon possessed.

From the before mentioned reasons, Jesus was justified when He was disappointed and angry with His disciples because of their inability to perform His commands. The question can be asked, would Jesus harbour the same expectations of current believers in the twenty first century to heal and deliver those in need as He expected of His disciples two thousand years ago when He sent them out to proclaim the gospel?" Honestly, the answer is yes![107] [108]

Seeing that His disciples were incapable of doing the job Jesus had to take matters into His own hands.

"And Jesus rebuked the devil; and he departed out of him: and the child was cured from that very hour. Then came the disciples to Jesus apart, and said, why could not we cast him out?" (Matthew 17: 18, 19)

The disciples were curious to find out why they could not drive out the evil spirit. They thought that they could deliver him and when they could not, they wanted to know why, so they asked Jesus. The answer that Jesus

---

[107] Maldonado, Guillermo. How to walk in the Supernatural Power of God. Whitaker House. 2011. Pg. 232
[108] Liardon, Roberts. God's Generals - Why they succeeded and why some failed. Albury Publishing. 1996. Pg. 276-277

gave them not only applied to them but also applies to most believers today. It is the chief reason why they failed then and believers today fail now. Before getting Jesus' answer let us see some of the excuses that believers use today as to why healing is not accomplished.

Four Explanations Believers Give for Failure

Four excuses believers give to explain why healing do not take place:

1. It is not God's will to heal the infirm person.

2. It might not be God's time to heal the person.

3. The sick person has sin in their life and this blocks God from healing the individual.

4. The sick person lacks faith.

To a point some of these reasons may have a certain amount of validity. For example, if a believer is not willing to confess and repent of sin in his life God may choose not to heal him. (James 5: 16)

However, let us think of the following. When an individual is not healed because it is not God's will or time, the blame is placed on God. If believers connect the lack of miraculous healing to the sick person's sins or absence of faith, then the ill person is blamed. The blame is being placed on God and/or the ill person when nothing happens after ministering to the sick. Believers never blame themselves when healing does not manifest after ministering to the afflicted.[109]

Jesus correctly attributed the fault of the unhealed boy to the disciples and not to God or the boy. It was because of their little faith and doubt, the boy was not healed. The absence of faith on the boy's part or the absence of God played no part in the unaccomplished miracle. There is a possibility that the boy did have sin in his life, but Jesus did not state this as the reason he was not delivered by the disciples.

When healing fails believers usually tend to blame God, sin or disbelief in the recipient. They fail to realize that they too could be at fault by their disbelief. Let us be reminded that the disciples failed to heal the boy not because they lacked authority, but they had disbelief and doubt. We are also reminded that it takes more than authority to manifest healing, it also takes faith of God.

> In addition, "To receive healing we must seek Christ, our healer... Not our healing. We must have our eyes fixed on Him, not upon someone else or upon certain preconceived ideas." Dr. Morris Cerullo. [110]

---

[109] Maldonado, Guillermo. Jesus Heals your sickness today. ERJ Publications.2009. Pg. 74-77

[110] Victory Miracle Library/Dr. Morris Cerullo – Pg 4, quoted with permission. Copyright 2000-2014 Morris Cerullo World Evangelism. All Rights Reserved. www.mcwe.com

Chapter Ten

Every Healing Command
Ever Issued By Jesus Christ

Throughout His ministry, Jesus spent countless hours in prayer and fasting. In doing so, He strengthened His faith in the priestly and kingly realm. Even though His prayer life had a direct effect on the miracles He preformed, He separated His prayer life from His miracles. During His miracles, there was no prayer. The only words that proceeded out of Jesus' mouth were direct commands to sickness, demons, death and forgiving the sins of the people. The following list is a compilation of authoritative commands (emboldened and underlined) issued by Jesus Christ throughout His ministry on earth as outlined in the four gospels.[111] [112] [113]

The Gospel of Matthew:

Matt 8: 3,7,13
3. "And Jesus put forth his hand, and touched him,

---

[111] THE NEW PROOF PRODUCERS / Dr. Morris Cerullo – Pg. 216-219, quoted with permission. Copyright 1998-2014 Morris Cerullo World Evangelism. All Rights Reserved. www.mcwe.com
[112] Lord Teach us to Pray/ Dr. Morris Cerullo – Pg. 207 – 224, quoted with permission. Copyright 2004-2014 Morris Cerullo World Evangelism. All Rights Reserved www.mcwe.com
[113] Maldonado, Guillermo. How to walk in the Supernatural Power of God. Whitaker House. 2011. Pg. 182-184

saying, **_I will; be thou clean_**. *And immediately his leprosy was cleansed.*

7. And Jesus saith unto him, **_I will come and heal him_**.

13. And Jesus said unto the centurion, **_Go thy way; and as thou hast believed, so be it done unto thee._** *And his servant was healed in the selfsame hour."*

Matt 8:32

32. "And he said unto them, **_Go_**. *And when they were come out, they went into the herd of swine: and, behold, the whole herd of swine ran violently down a steep place into the sea, and perished in the waters."*

Matt 9:6

6. "But that ye may know that the Son of man hath power on earth to forgive sins, (then saith he to the sick of the palsy,) **_Arise, take up thy bed, and go unto thine house."_**

Matt 9:22, 29

22. "But Jesus turned him about, and when he saw her, he said, **_Daughter, be of good comfort; thy faith hath made thee whole._** *And the woman was made whole from that hour.*

29. Then touched he their eyes, saying, __According__
__to your faith be it unto you.__"

Matt 10: 8

8. "__Heal the sick, cleanse the lepers, raise the__
__dead, cast out devils: freely ye have received, freely__
__give.__"

Matt 12: 13

13. "Then saith he to the man, __Stretch forth thine__
__hand__. And he stretched it forth; and it was restored
whole, like as the other."

Matt 15: 28

28. "Then Jesus answered and said unto her, __O__
__woman, great is thy faith: be it unto thee even as__
__thou wilt__. And her daughter was made whole from
that very hour."

The Gospel of Mark

Mark 1:25

25. "And Jesus rebuked him, saying, __Hold thy__
__peace, and come out of him__."

Mark 1:41

41. *"And Jesus, moved with compassion, put forth his hand, and touched him, and saith unto him, **I will; be thou clean**."*

Mark 2:11

11. *"**I say unto thee, Arise, and take up thy bed, and go thy way into thine house**."*

Mark 3: 3, 5

3. *"And he saith unto the man which had the withered hand, **Stand forth**.*

5. *And when he had looked round about on them with anger, being grieved for the hardness of their hearts, he saith unto the man, **Stretch forth thine hand**. And he stretched it out: and his hand was restored whole as the other."*

Mark 5: 8, 9, 34, 36, 41

8. *"For he said unto him, **Come out of the man, thou unclean spirit**.*

9. *And he asked him, **What is thy name?** And he answered, saying, My name is Legion: for we are many.*

34. And he said unto her, __Daughter, thy faith hath made thee whole; go in peace, and be__ whole __of thy plague.__

36. As soon as Jesus heard the word that was spoken, he saith unto the ruler of the synagogue, __Be not afraid, only believe.__

41. And he took the damsel by the hand, and said unto her, __Talitha cumi__; which is, being interpreted, __Damsel, I say unto thee, arise.__"

Mark 7:29, 34

29. "And he said unto her, __For this saying go thy way; the devil is gone out of thy daughter__.

34. "And looking up to heaven, he sighed, and saith unto him, __Ephphatha__, that is, Be opened."

Mark 9: 25

25. "When Jesus saw that the people came running together, he rebuked the foul spirit, saying unto him, __Thou dumb and deaf spirit, I charge thee, come out of him, and enter no more into him.__"

Mark 10: 52

52. "And Jesus said unto him, __Go thy way; thy faith__

hath made thee whole. *And immediately he received his sight, and followed Jesus in the way."*

Mark 16:17-18

17. "**_And these signs shall follow them that believe; In my name shall they cast out devils; they shall speak with new tongues;_**

18. **_They shall take up serpents; and if they drink any deadly thing, it shall not hurt them; they shall lay hands on the sick, and they shall recover._**"

The Gospel of Luke

Luke 4:35

35. *"And Jesus rebuked him, saying,* **_Hold thy peace, and come out of him_**. *And when the devil had thrown him in the midst, he came out of him, and hurt him not."*

Luke 5: 13, 24

13. *"And he put forth his hand, and touched him, saying,* **_I will: be thou clean_**. *And immediately the leprosy departed from him.*

24. *But that ye may know that the Son of man hath power upon earth to forgive sins, (he said unto the*

[144]

sick of the palsy,) I say unto thee, __Arise, and take up thy couch, and go into thine house.__"

Luke 6:8, 10

8. "But he knew their thoughts, and said to the man which had the withered hand, __Rise up, and stand forth in the midst.__ And he arose and stood forth.

10. And looking round about upon them all, he said unto the man, __Stretch forth thy hand__. And he did so: and his hand was restored whole as the other."

Luke 7: 14

14. "And he came and touched the bier: and they that bare him stood still. And he said, __Young man, I say unto thee, Arise.__"

Luke 8: 48, 50, 54

48. "And he said unto her, __Daughter, be of good comfort: thy faith hath made thee whole; go in peace.__

50. But when Jesus heard it, he answered him, saying, __Fear not: believe only, and she shall be made whole.__

54. *And he put them all out, and took her by the hand, and called, saying,* **Maid, arise**.*"*

Luke 10:9

9. **And heal the sick that are therein, and say unto them, The kingdom of God is come nigh unto you.***"*

Luke 13:12

12. *"And when Jesus saw her, he called her to him, and said unto her,* **Woman, thou art loosed from thine infirmity.***"*

Luke 17: 19

19. *"And he said unto him,* **Arise, go thy way: thy faith hath made thee whole.***"*

Luke 18: 42

42. *"And Jesus said unto him,* **Receive thy sight: thy faith hath saved thee**.*"*

The Gospel of John

John 4: 50

50. *"Jesus saith unto him,* **Go thy way; thy son liveth**. *And the man believed the word that Jesus*

had spoken unto him, and he went his way."

John 5: 8, 14

8. *"Jesus saith unto him,* **_Rise, take up thy bed, and walk_**.

14. *Afterward Jesus findeth him in the temple, and said unto him,* **_Behold, thou art made whole: sin no more, lest a worse thing come unto thee._**"

John 9: 7

7. *"And said unto him,* **_Go, wash in the pool of Siloam,_** *(which is by interpretation, Sent.) He went his way therefore, and washed, and came seeing."*

John 11: 43, 44

43. *"And when he thus had spoken, he cried with a loud voice,* **_Lazarus, come forth_**.

44. *And he that was dead came forth, bound hand and foot with grave clothes: and his face was bound about with a napkin. Jesus saith unto them,* **_Loose him, and let him go._**"

Chapter Eleven

Healing Commands and Gifts in the Book of Acts

- The Great Commission

Directed to the original twelve apostles or the present-day believer the commands were the same, go and show the world the much needed true sovereign power of Jesus. Believers today need to investigate the successful procedures that the early apostles used to prove their doctrine was the truth. One other crucial factor that must be realized is that God was with the disciples because they were obedient to Him. Their relationship with Him was strong and so they were given authority and it grew in them their faith of God. [114]

The early apostles were mandated by the Lord to continue to work the works of Jesus Christ. All believers in Christ for all generations were given the holy commission to lay hands on the sick and they shall recover. This is exactly what the early apostles did.

"And Jesus came and spake unto them, saying, All power is given unto me in heaven and in earth. Go

---

[114] THE NEW PROOF PRODUCERS / Dr. Morris Cerullo – Pg. 207, quoted with permission. Copyright 1998-2014 Morris Cerullo World Evangelism. All Rights Reserved. www.mcwe.com

ye therefore, and teach all nations, baptizing them in the name of the Father, and of the Son, and of the Holy Ghost: Teaching them to observe all things whatsoever I have commanded you: and, lo, I am with you alway, even unto the end of the world. Amen."

(Matthew 28:16-18)

Before Pentecost, the early disciples possessed divine authority to heal the sick and they proclaimed the Kingdom of God. It is very important to look at how the early Church moved in the realm of authority, as well as, when the gifts of healing was in operation. The Church is still living in the dispensation of Acts.[115]

The ministries of the apostles Peter and Paul will provide great insight of how these early fathers moved in the realm of authority and the gifts of healing. Following their example will help those who desire to walk in authority, power and the gifts of healing to flow in wisdom, knowledge and understanding in the twenty first century efficiently and effectively. All of the healing commands issued by the apostles are emboldened and underlined to stress the continuation of the pattern set forth by the Lord Jesus Christ.

---

[115] THE NEW PROOF PRODUCERS / Dr. Morris Cerullo – Pg 193, quoted with permission. Copyright 1998-2014 Morris Cerullo World Evangelism. All Rights Reserved. www.mcwe.com

Ministry Of Peter

Healing the Lame Beggar

Acts 3:1-10

1. *"Now Peter and John went up together into the temple at the hour of prayer, being the ninth hour.*

2. And a certain man lame from his mother's womb was carried, whom they laid daily at the gate of the temple which is called Beautiful, to ask alms of them that entered into the temple;

3. Who seeing Peter and John about to go into the temple asked an alms.

4. And Peter, fastening his eyes upon him with John, said, Look on us.

5. And he gave heed unto them, expecting to receive something of them.

*6. Then Peter said, **Silver and gold have I none; but such as I have give I thee: In the name of Jesus Christ of Nazareth rise up and walk.***

7. And he took him by the right hand, and lifted him up: and immediately his feet and ankle bones received strength.

8. And he leaping up stood, and walked, and entered with them into the temple, walking, and leaping, and praising God.

9. And all the people saw him walking and praising God:

10. And they knew that it was he which sat for alms at the Beautiful gate of the temple: and they were filled with wonder and amazement at that which had happened unto him."

It is important to note that Peter flowed in authority in his kingly office. He did not pray in tongues, he issued a command and performed an extraordinary miracle by healing a beggar who was lame from birth. His eyes were wide open when the command was given and authority in Jesus' name was exercised. At this point there was no use of the gifts of healing in operation. Peter did not direct any priestly action to his Heavenly Father.[116]

The Apostle Peter's shadow heals everyone

Acts 5: 12-16

12. "And by the hands of the apostles were many signs and wonders wrought among the people; (and they were all with one accord in Solomon's porch.

---

[116] THE NEW PROOF PRODUCERS / Dr. Morris Cerullo – Pg. 191, quoted with permission. Copyright 1998-2014 Morris Cerullo World Evangelism. All Rights Reserved. www.mcwe.com

13. And of the rest durst no man join himself to them: but the people magnified them.

14. And believers were the more added to the Lord, multitudes both of men and women.)

15. Insomuch that they brought forth the sick into the streets, and laid them on beds and couches, that at the least the shadow of Peter passing by might overshadow some of them.

16. There came also a multitude out of the cities round about unto Jerusalem, bringing sick folks, and them which were vexed with unclean spirits: and they were healed everyone."

Peter simply walked and wherever his shadow fell healing manifested. The gift of healing in this instance required very little effort. No authoritative command was given by the apostle Peter. This special gift upon Peter's life caused healing as well as deliverance for those who had unclean spirits. [117]

Peter Heals Aeneas

Acts 9: 34

*"And Peter said unto him, **Aeneas, Jesus Christ maketh thee whole: arise, and make thy bed.** And he arose immediately."*

---

[117] Maldonado, Guillermo. Jesus Heals your sickness today. ERJ Publications.2009. Pg. 123

Peter was travelling around the region visiting the saints of God. When he arrived at Lydda he came across Aeneas, a man who had been paralyzed for a period of eight years. Peter boldly stepped out in faith and commanded Aeneas to be healed in Jesus' name. [118] Peter issued an authoritative command. Peter was exercising his kingly office of authority. It must be noted that he did not speak in tongues, praise the Lord or worship. He simply released the command and it was done. Souls were saved as a result of this miraculous deed.

Peter Raises Dorcas from the Dead

Acts 9: 40

*"But Peter put them all forth, and **kneeled down, and prayed**; and turning him to the body said, **Tabitha, arise.** And she opened her eyes: and when she saw Peter, she sat up."*

This is the first time where two components were in operation: the priestly component in verse forty where Peter prayed followed by the kingly component of an authoritative command. [119]

---

[118] Trimm, Cindy. Commanding Your Morning. Charisma House. 2007. Pg. 138

[119] THE NEW PROOF PRODUCERS / Dr. Morris Cerullo – Pg. 192, quoted with permission. Copyright 1998-2014 Morris Cerullo World Evangelism. All Rights Reserved. www.mcwe.com

[154]

Although Scriptures does not tell us explicitly, it is very important to understand why on this occasion the apostle first prayed. This is not a matter of healing the sick. Dorcas is dead. There is a major difference from being sick and being dead. When someone is sick there is a ray of hope for healing and recovery. However, when someone has died, there is generally no more hope for that person on earth. The apostle was not dealing with sickness but was confronted by physical death itself.

Peter was mentored by Jesus Christ. He had been commanded by Jesus to raise the dead (Matthew 10: 8). Peter knew his authority; however, he was not quite ready to move this huge mountain which stood in his pathway to raise Dorcas back to life. He may have had some doubt; hence he spent quality time with his Heavenly Father first in the priestly office. As He sought the Lord in prayer, God prepared His apostle to move this mountain which stood in his pathway.

It is very important for believers to seek the Lord first like Peter, before embarking on raising the dead. Believers need to get the heart and mind of God through prayer first. Is it the will of God to bring this person back to life? This may have been Peter's prayer as he waited in God's presence to hear and the Father may have replied to him in the affirmative.

In addition to inquiring about the Lord's will, you might want to ask the Lord to increase your mountain-moving faith to move such a large mountain into the sea.

Apostles carry a high degree of authority in the realm of the spirit.[120] As a believer you may ask the Lord for the authority to raise the dead. This is a priestly action of going to the Lord on your face before the Father. You may offer praises, thanksgiving or worship to the Lord. You may even pray in the Holy Spirit building up your spiritual energy level as you roll the turbines in the spiritual realm (Jude 20). You will then be prepared to command the dead person with confidence to wake up in Jesus' Name.

It is important to note that as long as Peter was on his knees in prayer, the miracle did not manifest; Dorcas remained dead. You learn from this, that prayer in itself (apart from the gifts of healing) does not generally result in miraculous healings and the like. The purpose of prayer is divine preparation for performance in the miraculous through the use of authority. [121] [122]

When Peter put on his kingly robe and commanded the work of the enemy, whether it was death, a demon or infirmity to leave, he did it with authority and faith of God. At this point Peter no longer functioned in the priestly realm, but rather, fully stepped into his kingly authority.

---

[120] APOSTLES, PROPHETS AND THE COMING MOVES OF GOD/ Dr. Bill Hamon – Pg. 23-41, quoted with permission. Copyright 1997-2014 CHRISTIAN INTERNATIONAL MINISTRIES. All Rights Reserved. www.christianinternational.com

[121] Chavda, Mahesh. The Hidden Power Healing Prayer. Destiny Image Publishers, Inc. 2001. Pg. 115

[122] Maldonado, Guillermo. Jesus Heals your sickness today. ERJ Publications.2009.Pg 136-137

Peter stood up as a king, as one of God's generals in the army of the Lord and launched the missile of life directly into the physical body. He looked directly to the corpse and commanded her to arise. All of heaven and hell must obey the authority of God in a believer, who has sought the Father's approval first for raising the dead. It is extremely important to note that the priestly component is separated from the kingly function for effective ministry in raising the dead. Peter is exercising authority and not the gifts of healing. When Peter raised Dorcas back to life, this awesome miracle caused many in Joppa to believe in the Lord Jesus Christ. [123]

Ministry Of Paul

Authority to Cause Blindness on the Wicked

Acts 13: 6-12

6. "And when they had gone through the isle unto Paphos, they found a certain sorcerer, a false prophet, a Jew, whose name was Barjesus:

7. Which was with the deputy of the country, Sergius Paulus, a prudent man; who called for Barnabas and Saul, and desired to hear the word of God.

---

[123] Lord Teach us to Pray/ Dr. Morris Cerullo – Pg. 234, quoted with permission. Copyright 2004-2014 Morris Cerullo World Evangelism. All Rights Reserved www.mcwe.com

8. But Elymas the sorcerer (for so is his name by interpretation) withstood them, seeking to turn away the deputy from the faith.

9. Then Saul, (who also is called Paul,) filled with the Holy Ghost, set his eyes on him,

10. And said, O full of all subtilty and all mischief, thou child of the devil, thou enemy of all righteousness, wilt thou not cease to pervert the right ways of the Lord?

*11. **<u>And now, behold, the hand of the Lord is upon thee, and thou shalt be blind, not seeing the sun for a season</u>**. And immediately there fell on him a mist and a darkness; and he went about seeking some to lead him by the hand.*

12. Then the deputy, when he saw what was done, believed, being astonished at the doctrine of the Lord."

The apostle Paul exercised his kingly office by issuing a command against Elymas, who was seeking to hinder the word of the Lord from reaching the deputy. Paul used his kingly authority in an unorthodox way which brought salvation to the deputy when he saw the power of God manifested. The deputy believed in the Lord Jesus Christ and was amazed at the mighty demonstration of the power of God that caused blindness on Elymas.

Paul Heals a Lame Man at Lystra

Acts 14: 8-10

8. "And there sat a certain man at Lystra, impotent in his feet, being a cripple from his mother's womb, who never had walked:

9. The same heard Paul speak: who stedfastly beholding him, and perceiving that he had faith to be healed,

10. Said with a loud voice, **_Stand upright on thy feet._** *And he leaped and walked."*

The apostle Paul was not trained by the Lord Jesus Christ in the realm of using the authority of God to manifest divine healing. However, he clearly understood the underlying principles of authority and power in the Kingdom of God.

"And my speech and my preaching was not with enticing words of man's wisdom, but in demonstration of the Spirit and of power."

(1 Corinthians 2:4)

"To whom God would make known what is the riches of the glory of this mystery among the Gentiles; which is Christ in you, the hope of glory."

(Col. 1: 27)

[159]

The apostle Paul clearly understood it was the living Christ in him manifesting the hope of glory. He understood his calling in the ministry to demonstrate the kingdom of God in power and authority through the Holy Spirit. The Lord used him mightily to perform great signs, wonders and miracles.

When the apostle Paul came to Lystra, he recognized a man who had been a cripple from his mother's womb, but had the faith to be healed. Paul attired himself with his royal kingly robe of authority and issued an authoritative command with a loud voice. The result was a great miracle of healing with the man leaping and walking.[124]

Paul Casts Out a Spirit of Divination from a Damsel

Acts 16: 16-18

16. "And it came to pass, as we went to prayer, a certain damsel possessed with a spirit of divination met us, which brought her masters much gain by soothsaying:

17. The same followed Paul and us, and cried, saying, these men are the servants of the most high God, which shew unto us the way of salvation.

[124] THE NEW PROOF PRODUCERS / Dr. Morris Cerullo – Pg. 193, quoted with permission. Copyright 1998-2014 Morris Cerullo World Evangelism. All Rights Reserved. www.mcwe.com

18. And this did she many days. But Paul, being grieved, turned and said to the spirit, __I command thee in the name of Jesus Christ to come out of her__. And he came out the same hour."

Paul again exercised his kingly authority by commanding the demon to come out of the girl who was being used by men for soothsaying. He opened his eyes, turned towards her and spoke directly to the demon in the name of Jesus. It must be noted that the apostle Paul followed the exact guidelines set out by our Lord Jesus Christ. He didn't pray in tongues, worship and praise or even pray in his natural tongue. This should teach believers likewise who have never been taught by Jesus Christ to follow in sync with the same pattern as outlined in the Gospels, and that which the apostles and disciples followed in the Book of Acts. Paul was one of the greatest apostles who followed this set algorithm and received mighty breakthroughs and healings in the spiritual realm, as well as, mighty miracles of healing, deliverance and breakthrough in the natural realm.[125]

The Gifts of Healing – Special Miracles

Acts 19: 11-12

11. "And God wrought special miracles by the hands of Paul:

---

[125] Maldonado, Guillermo. Jesus Heals your sickness today. ERJ Publications.2009. Pg. 138-139

12. So that from his body were brought unto the sick handkerchiefs or aprons, and the diseases departed from them, and the evil spirits went out of them. "

Paul is not operating in the realm of his kingly office by issuing any authoritative commands to perform the fantastic miracles of healing and deliverance. What is in operation is not authority but the power of God Almighty working in this apostle's life. The apostle Paul was a chosen servant of God in who dwelt Jesus Christ through the Holy Spirit. Therefore the healing power, the *"dunamis"* which is in Christ, was also in Paul. This *"dunamis"* or power of God was actually transferred unto handkerchiefs or aprons. [126]

The healing power was transferred to the infirm and the demonized were set free when the handkerchiefs were placed on them. It was not *"exousia"* or authority that drove out the demons, but simply *"dunamis"* or power.[127] These were extraordinary miracles indeed. These miracles through Paul can be understood as the application of a simple principle which is already familiar through the transfer of healing power by the laying on of hands. [128]

---

[126] Thayer, Joseph H. Thayer's Greek-English Lexicon of the New Testament. Hendrickson Publishers. 2007. Pg. 158-159
[127] Maldonado, Guillermo. How to walk in the Supernatural Power of God. Whitaker House. 2011.Pg. 48-49
[128] Maldonado, Guillermo. Jesus Heals your sickness today. ERJ Publications.2009. Pg. 118-119

The John G. Lake Sermons on Dominion over Demons, Disease and Death quote:

> "The Spirit of God is just as tangible as electricity is. You handle it, you receive it from God through faith and prayer, your person becomes supercharged with it. The old apostle took handkerchiefs or aprons, held them in his hands until the handkerchiefs or aprons were supercharged with the Spirit of God. Then they were sent to the sick, the sick were healed and the demons were cast out of them." (Acts 19: 12) [129]

Eutychus is Raised from the Dead

Acts 20: 7-12

7. *"And upon the first day of the week, when the disciples came together to break bread, Paul preached unto them, ready to depart on the morrow; and continued his speech until midnight.*

8. *And there were many lights in the upper chamber, where they were gathered together.*

9. *And there sat in a window a certain young man named Eutychus, being fallen into a deep sleep: and as Paul was long preaching, he sunk down with sleep, and fell down from the third loft, and was taken up dead.*

---

[129] Lake, John G. <u>Sermons on Dominion over Demons, Disease and Death</u> . Christ for the Nations INC. 1949. Pg. 47

10. And Paul went down, and fell on him, and embracing him said, Trouble not yourselves; for his life is in him.

11. When he therefore was come up again, and had broken bread, and eaten, and talked a long while, even till break of day, so he departed.

12. And they brought the young man alive, and were not a little comforted."

The power of God was so strong upon Paul's life that the gift of raising the dead was flowing like a mighty river; there was no need for an authoritative command or even a word of prayer. He simply embraced the brother who had died from his long preaching and Eutychus was brought back to life. The resurrection life of Jesus Christ that was flowing through Paul simply was released into his body, soul and spirit and it quickened his mortal body. [130]

> *"And if the Spirit of him who raised Jesus from the dead is living in you, he who raised Christ from the dead will also give life to your mortal bodies because of his Spirit who lives in you."* (Romans 8: 11)

---

[130] RESURRECTION LIFE / Dr. Paul G. Trulin — Pg. 23-27, quoted with permission. Copyright 1983-2014 Moriah Publications Inc. All Rights Reserved. www.MoriahPublications.com

Paul Heals In Malta the Father of Publius and the Islanders

Acts 28: 1-10

1. "And when they were escaped, then they knew that the island was called Melita.

2. And the barbarous people shewed us no little kindness: for they kindled a fire, and received us every one, because of the present rain, and because of the cold.

3. And when Paul had gathered a bundle of sticks, and laid them on the fire, there came a viper out of the heat, and fastened on his hand.

4. And when the barbarians saw the venomous beast hang on his hand, they said among themselves, No doubt this man is a murderer, whom, though he hath escaped the sea, yet vengeance suffereth not to live.

5. And he shook off the beast into the fire, and felt no harm.

6. Howbeit they looked when he should have swollen, or fallen down dead suddenly: but after they had looked a great while, and saw no harm come to him, they changed their minds, and said that he was a god.

7. In the same quarters were possessions of the chief man of the island, whose name was Publius; who received us, and lodged us three days courteously.

8. And it came to pass, that the father of Publius lay sick of a fever and of a bloody flux: to whom Paul entered in, and prayed, and laid his hands on him, and healed him.

9. So when this was done, others also, which had diseases in the island, came, and were healed:

10. Who also honoured us with many honours; and when we departed, they laded us with such things as were necessary."

Paul performed two separate actions. First, he prayed to God. After the prayer, Paul laid his hands on Publius' father and healed him. Again, we see a familiar pattern: there was first prayer in the priestly office, which was separate and distinct from the actual action of healing the man. The action of healing took place through the laying on of Paul's hands. It is important to note that Paul did not issue an authoritative command in healing those on the island of Malta.

Chapter Twelve

Healing In the Twentieth / Twenty- First Century

Dr. Jenkins says, "Many people, in our modern society, try to tell us that God does not heal anymore; that the days of healing are past. May I let you in on a little secret?–Since God is a God of the NOW– Miracles are for the NOW! If God is the Lord, who changes not, (Malachi 3:6), and Jesus Christ is the same yesterday, today and forever (Hebrews 13:8), then healings and miracles are for us today. Would you agree? Friend, allow me to let you in on a little secret. The fallacy of healing and miracles not being for today is a lie from the father of lies, the devil."[131]

"Is it God's will to heal? Is it God's will to heal everyone or only a select few? Is it possible that sometimes it is God's will for sickness to affect us? Many denominations commonly teach that miracles and healing belong to the 'apostle era,' and that it ended when the last one died; hence, God no longer heals. This practice has submerged the people into

---

[131] Nineteen Gifts of God to His Children, by Dr. Terrence Jenkins, p.79. Copyright 1991, 48 HrBooks. Used by permission

an abyss of ignorance, making them susceptible to sickness." Guillermo Maldonado.[132]

There are conservative evangelical Christians who believe that the supernatural gifts of healing as described in 1 Corinthians 12 is no longer in operation in the twenty -first century.

"God can and does heal in response to prayer, but He does NOT work through so-called healers today with the same gifts of healing exercised by the apostles in the early church. We realize healing meetings are popular in many New Zealand churches today, but what goes on in those meetings is NOT the same as what went on in the New Testament." Timaru Bible Baptist Church[133]

However, John Eckhardt says, "Healing accompanies my Kingdom." [134] We know that God's kingdom has not vanished, therefore, healing has not vanished.

Whatever you believe about the gifts of healing, it will have little significance on what will be discussed. The

---

[132] Maldonado, Guillermo. Jesus Heals YOUR SICKNESS Today. ERJ Publicaciones. 2009. Pg. 15
[133] Timaru Bible Baptist Church. So you don't believe in divine healing either? < http://www.tbbc.co.nz/faq> Retrieved on 4/5/14
[134] Eckhardt, John. Daily Declarations for Spiritual Warfare. Charisma House.2011 Pg. 291

focus will be on something different which is far more foundational and applicable than the gifts of healing, something that will be strongly supported by the Word of God.

> Dr. Morris Cerullo says, "Christ intended for his church to know no limitations! He planned that we would be invincible and that His power would flow through us to fulfil His will and purpose on earth: proclaiming the Gospel, healing the sick, casting out demons, bringing in a worldwide harvest of souls and establishing his Kingdom on earth."[135]

> Dr. Morris Cerullo also declares, "What we believe is in a God of miracle working power who is alive in every day and every age. The days of miracles have never ceased because the God of miracles has never died" [136]

Some of God's great generals of the twentieth century, who moved in the authority and also gifts of healing are outlined in the contents of the book by Roberts Liardon.

> They are as follows: " John Alexander Dowie -The Healing Apostle, Maria Woodworth-Etter -

[135] Lord Teach us to Pray/ Dr. Morris Cerullo – Pg. 207, quoted with permission. Copyright 2004-2014 Morris Cerullo World Evangelism. All Rights Reserved www.mcwe.com

[136] THE NEW PROOF PRODUCERS / Dr. Morris Cerullo – Pg. 158, quoted with permission. Copyright 1998-2014 Morris Cerullo World Evangelism. All Rights Reserved. www.mcwe.com

Demonstrator of the Spirit, Evan Roberts - Welsh Revivalist, Charles F. Parham - The Father of Pentecost, William J. Seymour - The Catalyst of Pentecost, John G. Lake - A man of Healing, Smith Wigglesworth - Apostle of Faith, Aimee Semple McPherson - A Woman of Destiny, Kathryn Kuhlman - The Woman Who Believed in Miracles, William Branham - A Man of Notable Signs and Wonders, Jack Coe - The Man of Reckless Faith & A.A. Allen - The Miracle Man." [137]

It is important to ask the following questions:

1. How then does Jesus heal the sick today?

2. Who in this present age does the work that Jesus did when He was on earth?

It is important to look to the Word of God to get a clear understanding of the biblical perspective to answer these two questions.

1. How then does Jesus heal the sick today?

> *"I say unto you, He that believeth on me, the works that I do shall he do also; and greater works than these shall he do; because I go unto my Father."* *(John 14: 12)*

---

[137] Liardon, Roberts. God's Generals. Albury publishing. 1996. Pg. 9

Dr. Terrence Jenkins declares, "Therefore the ascension of Jesus did not mean an end to miracles, but rather an increase in the miraculous" [138]

While Jesus was on the earth, He did the following:

- He preached the gospel

- He made the sick whole

- He exorcised evil spirits

- He gave discipleship to the chosen

- *There was no supplication made for the sick*

Therefore, believers in Christ need to practice what Jesus did:

- Proclaim the word as Jesus did

- Bring healing to people as Jesus did

- Exorcise demons as Jesus did

- Give discipleship as Jesus did

Following in the footsteps of the King, His earthly kings must realize they are not going to be walking in the priestly realm of simply praying for the sick. His royal ones are going to heal the sick in the very same way that Jesus

---

[138] Jenkins, Terrence. Free Indeed. Publish America. 2006. Pg. 64

did while He was on this planet.[139] It must be noted that there is not one healing miracle in the gospel which was manifested as a result of Jesus praying to His Father. King Jesus always spoke with authority and the person would be healed. His earthly kings must learn to walk in the footsteps of Jesus.[140]

2. Who in this present age does the work that Jesus did while He was on earth?

Again, it is important to look to the Word of God to answer this question.

> *"Then he called his twelve disciples together, and gave them power and authority over all devils, and to cure diseases."* (Luke 9: 1)

Jesus handpicked twelve men to be His original apostles; the Father had given Jesus power and authority. Jesus in turn gave these men power and authority to drive out demons and to heal diseases and they walked as their earthly King walked: in mighty signs, wonders and miracles. [141]

What was the purpose of Jesus releasing divine authority in the hands of His apostles? The specific purpose

---

[139] Yohannan, K.P. A Journey of Perseverance. Send! Vol. 33 No. 2. The John Roberts Company. July, 2013.

[140] Wigglesworth, Smith. Smith Wigglesworth on Healing. Whitaker House. 1999. Pg. 50

[141] Maldonado, Guillermo. How to Receive and Minister Deliverance. ERJ Publications. November 2010 Pg. 21.

for which Jesus gave His apostles power and authority over diseases and demons was for preaching the Kingdom of God to the lost. The salvation of lost souls is the most important reason Christ came. [142] Hence, by His apostles demonstrating to the lost through signs, wonders and miracles, this would prove that Jesus was the promised Messiah.

Believers who want to learn to heal the sick using the authority that Jesus gave them must remember that the purpose and motivation must flow along the main artery of evangelism. Although the authority does work for ministering healing to believers, it is primarily meant for demonstrating to the world that Jesus Christ is the sovereign true God.[143]

"And he sent them to preach the kingdom of God, and to heal the sick." (Luke 9: 2)

According to Luke 9:2, Jesus instructs His disciples to go out with two distinct jobs. The first was to tell everyone about the good news of the Kingdom of God. The second command was to administer healing to those who needed it. The question stands, are these two instructions still valid and practiced in the twenty first century? The first of the two, which was to proclaim the good news of

---

[142] Tozer, A. W. The Root of the Righteous. Authentic Media. 2009. Pg. 47-49

[143] Woodwood-Etter, Maria. Signs, and Wonders. Whitaker House.1997. Pg. 186

the kingdom of God, is clearly still in practice.[144] The second, to administer healing to those who need it, is debatable in many churches.[145] However, if healing is administered according to the guidelines set by Jesus Christ, healing will take place. It was not negated or limited after the death of the twelve apostles. It is still valid in the twenty- first century to all those who dare to practice commanded healing in Jesus' name. [146]

The churches of today are filled with ministers proclaiming the Kingdom of God and the gospel of Jesus Christ. Yet, they have fallen short in the second command which involves healing the sick and setting the captives free from demonic possession. What is needed in the church is complete repentance for being disobedient to Jesus' command and following the guidelines in which He set forth pertaining to healing.[147]

This involves a paradigm shift in alignment to what the Word of God teaches and the stratagems outlined in chapters ten and eleven. The administration of healing is firmly grounded in the teachings of Jesus which are found in the gospels and in Acts. Over the past two thousand

---

[144] Tozer, A. W. Man: The Dwelling Place of God. Authentic Media. 2009. Pg. 139-142

[145] Timaru Bible Baptist Church. So you don't believe in divine healing either? < http://www.tbbc.co.nz/faq> Retrieved on 4/5/14

[146] Jenkins, Terrence. Nineteen Gifts of God to His Children. 48HrBooks. 1991.Pg. 78-81

[147] Bosworth, F.F. Christ The Healer. Fleming H. Revell. 1973. Pg. 175

years, the Church has detoured from Jesus' teaching with regards to healing the infirm.[148]

With regards to our present pattern, the command for believers to heal the sick seems out of this world. How can believers be commanded to do something that only Almighty God has the power and authority to do? Believers can try to heal the sick, but how can they minister healing as Jesus did? These questions will be answered later, but for now, consider this. It does not matter if God commands us to do something "natural" like clothing the destitute or something "supernatural" like healing cancer. If He commands us to do it, clearly He will equip us with the power and authority to do it successfully.[149]

When it comes to healing the sick most believers today fail miserably. There are two possible reasons why this happens. Some believers were never taught that they possessed the authority to command healing in Jesus' name. Others know they have the authority yet are afraid of using it because of the high-risk of fear of failing, so they limit themselves to saying a prayer for the sick individual. This is a devastating blow to proclaiming the Gospel and the Kingdom of God because Jesus used these healings as evidence of the existence of the Kingdom of God.[150]

---

[148]The Eternal Church / Dr. Bill Hamon — Pg. 93, quoted with permission. Copyright 2003-2014 CHRISTIAN INTERNATIONAL MINISTRIES. All Rights Reserved. www.christianinternational.com

[149] Eckhardt, John. Daily Declarations for Spiritual Warfare: Biblical Principles to   Defeat the Devil. Charisma Media. 2011. Pg. 166

The Contrast between Praying and Commanding Healing In Jesus' Name

Praying for the sick is simply asking God to heal the individual in need of ministry. If the person is healed, believers praise and thank the Lord. If the person is not healed, believers still worship God and know that it is not God's will. Believers have not failed if the person is still sick after supplication to God because God is Supreme. His answers can be 'yes/no' to our prayer. The believer's job is simply to ask (Matt 7:7); it is God's decision to heal. Praying for the sick is risk free. Believers are not accountable for the results. It does not require much to pray for the infirmed.[150]

This will completely revolutionize the entire structure of the known Church if they were to ever grasp the full understanding of the methods used by Jesus Christ.

Within the church there is healing the sick by faith which is a common practice. Within different circles in the Body of Christ, there are varied understandings of the meaning of "healing the sick." Some believe that healing the sick is completely a matter of faith according to Mark 11: 24 which states:

---

[150] Lord Teach us to Pray/ Dr. Morris Cerullo – Pg. 165 – 166, quoted with permission. Copyright 2004-2014 Morris Cerullo World Evangelism. All Rights Reserved www.mcwe.com

"Therefore I say unto you, What things soever ye desire, when ye pray, believe that ye receive them, and ye shall have them."

According to this understanding, after the believer asks God in prayer to heal someone, the believer believes that the person is healed and the person will in fact be healed. Then the believer just praises and thanks God for the healing of the individual.[151]

Healing the Sick by Faith

Imagine the following scenario. A believer enters an unreached village in the country of Guyana where witchcraft has complete dominance over the people. As a believer, you gather the people together and tell them about the redeeming blood of Jesus. The disbelievers already know about the supernatural power of witchcraft, the disbelievers ask you to demonstrate the mighty power of your God as a believer. They bring a sick child in great pain petitioning you to heal the infirmed. This is the very context for which Jesus gave power and authority to His disciples and commanded them to use it to heal the sick. Using the action of faith, the believer after prayer, lays hands on the child and declares, "Be healed in the name of Jesus Christ." Because the believer believes that the child is

---

[151] The Miracle Book (How you can live in a rhythm of miracles using 5 simple steps) / Dr. Morris Cerullo – Pg. 88-89, quoted with permission. Copyright 1998-2014 Morris Cerullo World Evangelism. All Rights Reserved. www.mcwe.com

healed, the individual declares before the assembled villagers, "Praise God, this child is healed by faith! By faith he is now completely free from pain!"

All eyes are fastened on the child. However, the pain has not subsided one iota and the child is in great anguish. The question arises, has the individual healed the child as Jesus healed the sick two thousand years ago? Is this the kind of healing Jesus commanded His disciples when He sent them out to proclaim the kingdom of God? Are the villagers who witnessed this "miracle" now convinced that Jesus Christ is greater than the pain the child experienced and will they decide to repent of their sins?

Jesus did not use the principle of healing by faith that is confessing healing before it actually happened or with no visible results, but rather demonstrated the power of God to perform miracles of healing. The afflicted were *actually* healed, most times immediately, proving that He was the Messiah. The definition of healing as Jesus commanded His disciples is not what is practiced by some churches and believers today.[152]

Faith healing can have a place when ministering to afflicted believers for the purpose of building the Body of Christ. But, it is *not* what Jesus commanded His disciples to do when evangelizing the lost.[153]

---

[152] Chavda, Mahesh. The Hidden Power Healing Prayer. Destiny Image Publishers, Inc. 2001. Pg. 107-110

Healing the Sick As Jesus Did

Manifestations of healing include: complete restoration of sight to the blind, complete restoration of hearing to the deaf; it gives rise to people giving evidence that they have been miraculously healed. Divine healing has not taken place when someone simply claims their healing "by faith" despite the continuation of their symptoms.[153]

The possibility of failure to produce the same healing results as Jesus did is ever present. After all we are not Jesus but regular human beings. Many believers today have tried to reproduce the results of Jesus Christ where healing is concerned and most times have not been able to do so.

For example, you may have once tried to heal someone's pain resulting from a toothache. You laid your hand on their jaw and rebuked the pain in Jesus' name. Then you asked him how he felt. To your surprise and dismay, he admitted that the pain doubled after you laid hands on him. You still remember how you felt after hearing those words. It was embarrassing and you felt horrible. Imagine how this horrible feeling is greatly multiplied when a failed healing occurs in a huge crowd that you are preaching the gospel to. Healing is not one hundred percent guaranteed, there is a certain level of risk.

---

[153] Maldonado, Guillermo. Jesus heals your sickness today. ERJ Publications.2009.Pg. 137

It doesn't always "work." Since you are the physical contact for the administration of healing the sick in Jesus' Name, you feel a certain measure of responsibility in determining the outcome. When nothing happens, you feel part of the reason for the failure could be you. Therefore, you reason it is much easier and less nerve-wracking to stay within your comfort zone and pray for the sick than to heal the sick as Jesus commanded His disciples.[154]

The fact that most church members were never taught that they have the ability/authority to heal the sick, coupled with doubt and fear of the risk of failure, explains why the church rarely heals the sick and why they are contented with just praying for the sick. It is now common practice, to pray to God to heal the sick and say that God will heal them in his timing and according to his divine will and purpose for their lives. Although these words have a wonderful spiritual twist they do not come in agreement with what Jesus commanded concerning the healing of the afflicted. Most of the times the long-winded and eloquent prayers for healing of some believers are simply a facade that masks the underlying fear and doubts of unsuccessful divine healing. [155]

Preaching the Gospel and Healing People Everywhere

---

[154] Maldonado, Guillermo. How to walk in the Supernatural Power of God. Whitaker House. 2011. Pg. 192-193
[155] Chavda, Mahesh. The Hidden Power Healing Prayer. Destiny Image Publishers, Inc. 2001. Pg. 58-59

"And they departed, and went through the towns, preaching the gospel, and healing everywhere." (Luke 9: 6)

Proclaiming the gospel of Jesus Christ and divine healing are intertwined. Human beings are drawn to miraculous manifestations as a direct result of our human nature[156]. It is for this reason that Jesus used the miraculous to expose the kingdom of God and his unconditional love to the disbelievers.[157]

"Then said Jesus unto him, Except ye see signs and wonders, ye will not believe." (John 4: 48)

Heal the Sick, Raise the Dead, Cast Out Demons

"And when he had called unto him his twelve disciples, he gave them power against unclean spirits, to cast them out, and to heal all manner of sickness and all manner of disease." (Matthew 10: 1)

As previously stated above, both Matthew and Luke refer in their writings to the same incident with similar perspectives. Jesus gathered His twelve disciples together privately and bestowed upon them authority to heal all manner of sickness, diseases and to cast out devils.

---

[156] Maldonado, Guillermo. Jesus heals your sickness today. ERJ Publications.2009. Pg. 127

[157] Maldonado, Guillermo. How to walk in the Supernatural Power of God. Whitaker House. 2011. Pg. 14

Therefore a valid conclusion can be made that the apostles did have the level of authority needed to heal the sick.

> *"And as ye go, preach, saying, The kingdom of heaven is at hand. Heal the sick, cleanse the lepers, raise the dead, cast out devils: freely ye have received, freely give."* *(Matthew 10: 7, 8)*

It is necessary to distinguish that Jesus commanded His disciples to heal the sick, not pray for the sick, to exorcise a demonic entity from an individual and not pray for that individual, to raise the dead and not pray for the dead. [158]

Why Are Miraculous Healings Rare In The Church Today?

Divine healing is not being taught in the churches today. In some churches, divine healing is seen as not religious, but as the work of negative forces.[159] Simply put, some churches have decided not to follow Jesus' commandment concerning divine healing.[160]

---

[158] THE NEW PROOF PRODUCERS / Dr. Morris Cerullo – Pg. 229, quoted with permission. Copyright 1998-2014 Morris Cerullo World Evangelism. All Rights Reserved. www.mcwe.com

[159] So What's The Difference, by Fritz Ridenour, p.125. Copyright 2001, Gospel Light/Regal Books, Ventura, CA 93003. Used by permission. 125

"My people are destroyed for lack of knowledge: because thou hast rejected knowledge..." (Hosea 4: 6)

What about Disciples Who Are Not Apostles?

There is a distinction between a believer and an apostle. A believer is someone who believes in Jesus Christ, an apostle is a committed and unyielding believer in Christ. He/she goes the extra mile and follows the commands of Jesus Christ without compromise.[160] It must be noted that in Luke 9 and Matthew 10, Jesus specifically gave power and authority over diseases and demons to the twelve apostles. The question arises, is every believer of Christ endowed with such power and authority or was it limited to the apostles?

"After these things the Lord appointed other seventy also, and sent them two and two before his face into every city and place, whither he himself would come." (Luke 10: 1)

(Some Bible translations say the Lord appointed seventy two disciples)

Here we see Jesus delegating authority to seventy regular disciples, not apostles and sending them out as fore-runners to preach the gospel and the Kingdom of God to his future

---

[160] The Day of The Saints / Dr. Bill Hamon — Pg. 21, 192, quoted with permission. Copyright 2002-2014 CHRISTIAN INTERNATIONAL MINISTRIES. All Rights Reserved. www.christianinternational.com

destinations. In addition to this delegation Jesus also gave these seventy nameless disciples the same power and authority to heal the sick and cast out demons.[161]

> *"And heal the sick that are therein, and say unto them, the Kingdom of God is come nigh unto you." (Luke 10: 9)*

This evidence suggests that Jesus did not limit the power and authority over sicknesses and demonic entities to just the apostles but rather to every disciple or believer.

It Is the Lord's Will to Heal the Sick When the Gospel Is Being Proclaimed

Humans at times contemplate the will of God concerning divine healing. It is during these times that contemplation negatively affects the healing process resulting in an unhealed individual. It is absolutely necessary to address this issue before any healing takes place. If it is not in the will of God to heal a certain individual that person will not be healed.[162]

---

[161] THE NEW PROOF PRODUCERS / Dr. Morris Cerullo – Pg. 229-234, quoted with permission. Copyright 1998-2014 Morris Cerullo World Evangelism. All Rights Reserved. www.mcwe.com

[162] Lake, John G, Lindsay, Gordon. The John G. Lake Sermons on Dominion over Demons, Disease and Death. Christ for the Nations Inc. 1949. Pg. 114-118

For the purpose of proclaiming the Kingdom of God to the lost there is Biblical evidence to uphold this statement; it is indeed God's will to perform miraculous healings.

Luke 9: 11

"And the people, when they knew *it*, followed him: and he received them, and spake unto them of the kingdom of God, and healed them that had need of healing."

If Jesus instructed His disciples to heal the sick, the conclusion can be drawn that it is His will for the sick to be healed. The purpose of healing the sick was to draw the attention of the lost to Him being the Messiah while bringing the Kingdom of God to the people. When the Lord tells believers to heal the sick, it is more than obvious to conclude that it is His will for the sick to be healed. [163]

"And the seventy returned again with joy, saying, Lord, even the devils are subject unto us through thy name." (Luke 10:17)

---

[163] Maldonado, Guillermo. Jesus heals your sickness today. ERJ Publications.2009. Pg. 15

The authority the disciples received from Jesus was not limited only to physical ailments and medical conditions, but rather all demonic entities residing in individuals.[164]

Why Only A Measure of Power and Authority?

Compared to the average believer an apostle may have a higher degree or level of divine power and authority. However, authority that is granted from the Lord is like money that an employer entrusts to his employee. If a believer is faithful with the little that he has, the Lord will increase the degree of authority to that believer. Believer's faithfulness and righteousness will be tested by God at each level, if they pass the test they will increase from that level of authority to a higher level.[165] (See Matt 25:14-30)

Conclusion

When Jesus bestowed power and authority over diseases, demonic entities and death, He did not only reserve it for the twelve apostles, but He gave it freely to the additional seventy disciples that He sent out as well. [166] A certain amount of power and authority was given to each disciple and/or apostle to do the work that Jesus entrusted

---

[164]The New Testament Church in Today's World / Dr. Paul G. Trulin — Pg. 125, quoted with permission. Copyright 1987-2014 Moriah Publications Inc. All Rights Reserved. www.MoriahPublications.com

[165] THE NEW PROOF PRODUCERS / Dr. Morris Cerullo – Pg. 213-219, quoted with permission. Copyright 1998-2014 Morris Cerullo World Evangelism. All Rights Reserved. www.mcwe.com.

[166] THE NEW PROOF PRODUCERS / Dr. Morris Cerullo – Pg. 207-212, quoted with permission. Copyright 1998-2014 Morris Cerullo World Evangelism. All Rights Reserved. www.mcwe.com.

these individuals with. Every born-again believer is in fact a disciple of Jesus Christ, therefore it can be concluded that every born-again believer can receive an amount of power and authority over sickness and demonic entities. Furthermore, the amount of power and authority a believer receives has the potential to grow based on the believer's obedience, faithfulness and righteousness to Jesus Christ.[167]

[167] Ibojie, Cynthia & Joe. Times of Refreshing, Volume Two. Cross House Books. 2012. June 27th

Chapter Thirteen

Healing and the
Faith of the Afflicted

Sickness is a trial of our patience and of our endurance.[168] But more than all this, sickness is a trial of our faith. In considering a connection between faith and healing, a common belief is that if you have faith, God will always heal you and if you do not have faith, He will not. So people have come to the conclusion that if God does heal someone, that person must have had faith.

Based on this reasoning, healing and non-healing can become evidence of righteousness or sinfulness. We have seen cases in which God did not heal even faith filled people like Elisha who healed many and raised a boy from the dead.[169] He healed some with little or no faith, and it seems that God sometimes heals regardless of faith, simply to extend His mercy to a suffering person.

The equation drawn by some that those who are healed always have greater faith than those who are not, is false. The biblical facts tell us that faith and obedience are

---

[168] Chavda, Mahesh. The Hidden Power Healing Prayer. Destiny Image Publishers, Inc. 2001. Pg. 114-115

[169] Accepting Christ, Your Healer / Dr. Morris Cerullo - Pg. 32-35, quoted with permission. Copyright 2010-2014 Morris Cerullo World Evangelism. All Rights Reserved. www.mcwe.com

not the total explanation but rather, God's will for the person, takes precedence. [170]

God Decides What Is Best

At times, our prayers may affect or even alter God's will within certain limits.[171] But a sick individual should not want his will to override God's judgment, which is always better than ours. The sick person should pray for healing, according to God's will, as Christ did when He asked that His cup of suffering be removed.

Jesus said "… nevertheless not my will but thine be done." (Matthew 26: 36 – 45)

The Father did not remove the suffering. You must have the understanding that God has not failed you if you are not healed.[172]

Absolute Trust in God

One of the most noted examples of faith in the Bible is the story of Shadrach, Meshach and Abednego in the fiery furnace (Daniel 3). These three Hebrew boys refused to

---

[170] Maldonado, Guillermo. Jesus heals your sickness today. ERJ Publications.2009. Pg. 15-22
[171] Seasons of Intercession / Frank Damazio- Pg. 99-109, quoted with permission. Copyright 1998-2014 City Christian Publishing. All Rights Reserved. www.CityChristianPublishing.com
[172] Made Alive / Dr. Charles S. Price co. Dr. Paul G. Trulin — Pg. 68-71, quoted with permission. Copyright 1945-2014 Moriah Publications Inc. All Rights Reserved. www.MoriahPublications.com

bow to the King's image and had bold faith that their God would deliver them. As we know, God delivered them alive from the fire.

Why Does God Allow Suffering?

The Bible makes clear that God allows suffering in this life, in order to build character (1 Peter 1:7). All the righteous, including Abraham, Sarah, Moses, David, Job and the apostles, suffered to different degrees at one time or the other. Christians cannot judge what will happen in their lives by what happens to another (2 Corinthians 10:12). Some Christians may never be healed. Others may be ill but may receive immediate healing.

What Does The Bible Say About Medical Sciences?

Should a Christian visit a medical doctor and seek his services? Does the Bible ban the use of medicine? God has not commanded Christians to avoid doctors, nor to refuse medicines, blood transfusions or surgery.[173]

In Genesis 17:10–14, God ordained a minor surgery for Abraham, in the procedure of circumcision. Physicians are called Joseph's "servants" in Genesis 50:2. The word for physician here is the same word used for God as healer in Exodus 15:26.

---

[173] Sandford, John, Paula. Healing The Wounded Spirit. Victory house INC. 1985. Pg. 75-102

Medicine is mentioned in Proverbs 17:22 as *"A merry heart does good like a medicine,"* and here, medicine is used in a positive way.[174]

Jeremiah 51:8 says that medicine is the way for Babylon to be healed. Although these examples are metaphors, they suggest that medicines are useful.

Ezekiel 47:12 shows healing medicine will be made from the leaves of trees that are nourished by waters from the new temple in the New Jerusalem.[175] Revelation 22:2 alludes to this. Luke 5:31 records Jesus' statement, *"Those who are well do not need a physician, but those who are sick."* Further in Luke 4: 23, Jesus says, *"Physician, heal yourself",* and applied it to himself. So there is no indication that Christ disproves of physicians.

Colossians 4: 14 state that Luke was called the "Beloved physician." So based on these Biblical examples, no one can come to the conclusion that the Bible in anyway condemns doctors or medicine.

However, physicians are merely mortal humans and can work only with the laws God designed to speed up or aid recovery. God never condemned that. Healing is not a test of righteousness; neither is visiting a doctor a test of righteousness. It does not show a lack of faith in God's

---

[174] Reynolds, Joshua. 20/20 Brain Power. 20/20 Brain Power Partners LLC. 2005. Pg. 3

[175] Rubin, Jordan S. The Maker's Diet. Siloam. 2005. Chapter 11

ability to heal; neither does it stop God from performing a miracle. [176]

Taking Personal Responsibility

In any trial, whether it is sickness, the primary responsibility for decisions and actions rests on the sick person or another responsible adult in the case of an under-aged individual. Each of us has been given a body by God and by so doing, He charges us with the responsibility to take care of our health. [177] Steps include: resting properly, exercise and a balanced diet. But even a person, who has taken all the cautionary measures to ensure good health, will probably get sick one or more times.

> "If we ever hope to be counted among the world's healthiest people, we must leave behind our disease-producing diets and lifestyle and return to our Creator's dietary guidelines, as incorporated in the Maker's Diet!"[178] -Jordan S Rubin.

Calling For the Elders of the Church

> *"Is anyone among you sick? Let him call for the elders of the church, and let them pray over him,*

---

[176] Bosworth, F.F. Christ The Healer. Fleming H. Revell. 1973. Pg. 194-196

[177] My Body His Life / Dr. Paul G. Trulin — Pg. 149-159, quoted with permission. Copyright 1993-2014 Moriah Publications Inc. All Rights Reserved. www.MoriahPublications.com

[178] Rubin, Jordan. THE MAKER'S DIET. Siloam.2005. Pg.49

anointing him with oil in the name of the Lord. And the prayer of faith will cure those being sick, and the Lord will raise him up. And if he may have committed sin, it will be forgiven him. Confess faults to one another, and pray for one another, that you may be healed. The prayer of a righteous one has great strength, having been made effective."

(The Interlinear Bible, James 5:14-16)[179]

Does this scripture suggest that everyone will be healed by God every time they go before the elders of the Church? Although the statement, "and the Lord will raise him up" initially appears to be written without substantiation, it sits amongst the rest of the Bible and is qualified by the rest of the Bible. Every verse in the Bible must be read in the context of the whole Bible and not be isolated. The meaning of each verse would be completely different when looked at from these two perspectives.

Here, as in every other case of a request for answered prayer, is the implied condition of healing being *in the best interest* of the party. It is an implied condition, but it is stated in the Bible to apply to all prayer.

"If we ask anything according to His will, He hears us" (1 John 5:14).

---

[179] Green, Jay. P. Sr. The Interlinear Bible, Hebrew-Greek- English. Hendrickson Publishers. 2008.

The Greek word "sózó" that is used sparingly in the Bible with reference to a person being made well from sickness (e.g., Mark 6:56). [180] According to The Thayer's Greek-English Lexicon of the New Testament the word "sózó" means the following: bring...safely, cured, ensure salvation, get well, made well, preserved, recover, restore, save, saved, saves and saving. [181]

Contrary to what some people believe, for an individual to call the doctor first and then the elders second, is often the wise thing to do and does not necessary show more faith in humans than in God. It simply shows common sense when faced with an emergency. Humans take a longer time to react than God does so they need to be contacted first. First aid should be administered first before calling an elder. Rendering self-help or medical aid does not necessarily show a lack of faith in God.

The Church's Responsibility

The primary responsibility of the church is to impart the truth about divine healing and to give spiritual counsel and encouragement through its ministries. It is not the responsibility of the church to take any position for or against any particular health therapy or procedure, except

---

[180] Wigram, George V. The Englishman's Greek Concordance of the New Testament. Hendrickson Publishers. 2006. Pg. 716

[181] Thayer, Joseph H. Thayer's Greek-English Lexicon of the New Testament. Hendrickson Publishers. 2007. Pg. 610

to recommend that any care sought, should be the best available and affordable.[182]

Conclusion

Sickness is the malfunction of one's body. Divine healing is God's divine and supernatural intervention to resolve such a problem. Factors to determine if God will heal include faith and God's will in our life. Using the service of medical doctors, as well as the use of medicine, is not a sin but a blessing.[183]

[182] Woodwood-Etter, Maria. Signs, and Wonders. Whitaker House.1997. Pg. 188-189
[183] Rubin, Jordan S. The Maker's Diet. Siloam. 2005. Pg. 178

Chapter Fourteen

Activations for Distance Healing Of Multiple Individuals

Dr. Morris Cerullo declares, "Faith Is A Fact, But Faith Is An Act!"[184]

In spite of having all the theory of divine healing, it is extremely important that believers in Christ be activated in their kingly dimension as Jesus was. Activation is simply putting into practice what you have learnt.

Below are the guidelines of activation in Ministering Spiritual Gifts according to Christian International in the realm of the prophetic. However, the same principles can be applied to the activation of the saints in the instruction of the protocols of Divine Healing.

Activation Guidelines:

1.   Creating The Proper atmosphere

As a leader, one of your goals is to create a friendly environment that encourages faith. To accomplish that:

a.   Don't rebuke publicly.

---

[184] THE MIRACLE BOOK / Dr. Morris Cerullo – Pg. 76, quoted with permission. Copyright 1984-2014 Morris Cerullo World Evangelism. All Rights Reserved. www.mcwe.com

b.   Public correction should be with the utmost tact.

c.   Communicate with encouragement. Make the people feel comfortable and relaxed.

d.   Humour is one way to keep people **relaxed.** ** Use the method that is best for you.

e.   On the whole, students give quality prophetic words. Make the congregation aware of this frequently. Your attitude should be, "See how easy that was. You accurately express the heart and mind of the Father!"

**What We Mean By "Relaxed"- During activation times your intent should be to produce an atmosphere of peace, joy, faith, trust, and confidence. As people become tense and fearful, they can hinder their own ability to receive from the Holy Spirit.

2.   **Any Minister Can Activate**

Any five-fold minister can activate the saints. However, some will have a greater effectiveness developing a mature exercise of the gifts in the individual saints.

3.   **Periodically Share Activation Guidelines With Your People**

Say things like:

a.   *This is a special time and place for this. Don't do it elsewhere without proper oversight.*

b.   *Don't make any major decisions on a prophetic word you receive in an activation time. Allow God to confirm independently by established ministers and wise counsel.*

c.   *Write out your word as soon as possible. Keep it in a notebook with the rest of your prophecies.*

d.   *Counsel with your pastor/elder about all words you receive.*

e.   *Seek to edify the body when ministering spiritual gifts.*

f.   *Be teachable.*

g.   *Flow with the order of the service.*

h.   *Give <u>personal</u> words only under pastoral supervision.*

4.   **When To Activate**

We find the best times to allow Saints to exercise their gifts are: (1) after the worship, and (2) after the message.

You can also activate the Saints in any type of service: Sunday morning, Sunday night, mid-week service, Sunday school, and home group meetings (assuming someone is present who is capable of providing proper oversight). It is unwise to activate the Saints when no one is present to oversee the activation and provide spiritual covering.

Don't hesitate to activate the Saints in the weeks and months following salvation. Don't wait for them to be "Holy" or "mature" enough to move in the gifts. Spiritual gifts are GIFTS. They are not earned. By activating the Saints early in their Christian experience, you will allow God to begin using them in their area of anointing. Ministering brings a very rewarding, fulfilling dimension to their Christian walk. Activating saints early in their spiritual growth will give them stability and depth as they do the will of God.

5.   E.S.S. and E.S.G not E.S.P.

This manual is based on the premise that practice is vital to the proper performance. Hence, you are teaching your students to **Exercise Spiritual Senses and Exercise Spiritual Gifts -** Not to use extra sensory perception, mind control, psychic ability, etc. We practice with fellow students because it is easier to perceive a spiritual thought (word from the Lord) for another rather than for oneself. Attempting to practice exclusively upon oneself creates potential hindrances such as personal conviction, mind-sets, and soul-blockage."[185]

Activation # 1: Healing from a distance to those with pain.

For the comfort of practice, use a safe place like a church setting with believers. Ask all those with pain in their bodies to stand. Then ask them to lay hands on the affected area for themselves as a point of contact. As the minister of healing, you can say, "Pain go now in Jesus' Name and never return!" Ask all those that are standing to check if there is any pain. Those who receive their healing let them come forward and testify by giving God all the glory. Command a second, third, fourth, fifth, sixth and seventh time until all the pain within the afflicted lives leaves in Jesus' Name.[186]

Activation # 2: Healing of heart conditions from a distance

---

[185] Manual For Ministering Spiritual Gifts / Dr. Bill Hamon – Pg. 7, 8, quoted with permission. Copyright 2004-2014 Christian International Ministries Network. All Rights Reserved. www.christianinternational.com

[186] Maldonado, Guillermo. Jesus heals your sickness today. ERJ Publications.2009. Pg. 141

Ask all those who have friends or relatives in need of healing of the heart to come forward. Ask them if they can possibly make a cell call to the afflicted person with the heart condition. When the call is made, then the one ministering divine healing should issue commands and then ask the believers to repeat the commands as follows: "Heart be healed now in Jesus' Name. Be restored now in Jesus' Name! Hearts be made whole right now in Jesus' Name." After the command is made, let them now ask the recipient how they are feeling. It is very important to always test and if possible for them to visit a doctor to confirm their healing through the authority in Jesus' Name.[187]

Activation # 3: Healing Alignment of Back, Spine and Extremities.

Ask all those who have misaligned backs and spines to come forward. In this activation, you will literally see the power of God as it changes the configuration of the bones and the spine and the Lord releases the miraculous instantly. Let the afflicted sit in chairs and then ask those sitting to stretch out their legs. The person ministering healing at a distance should issue a command such as: "Bones, feet, legs and spine be aligned now in the Name of Jesus." [188]

---

[187] Maldonado, Guillermo. Jesus heals your sickness today. ERJ Publications.2009. Pg. 161-162

[188] Rambally, Rohan. Prophetic Miracles Part 1. www.youtube.com. 7/19/12 <http://www.youtube.com/watch?v=ZTFbIqH-pO0>

These activations were all done and are posted on YouTube for the benefit of the Body of Christ to perform miracles, signs and wonders like Jesus Christ.

As a believer in Jesus Christ, you are able to accomplish great breakthroughs in ministering healing at a distance like Jesus Christ. With today's technology there is no distance or barrier in ministering healing at a distance. Recently, I ministered healing at a distance to a young woman in New York who had been in a major car accident via Skype.

The commands which were issued were, "Pain be gone and bones be aligned in Jesus' Name." When the young woman went back to the chiropractor the bones were perfectly aligned. The young woman gave God all the glory for healing at a distance.

Always remind the recipients to give God all the glory!

Chapter Fifteen

Testimonials

The following are present-day examples of testimonials by individuals who have received divine healing by God through myself and others.

Testimonial One:

Miraculous Healing of Cancer

"Not long ago, Apostle Maldonado traveled with his ministry team to bring the supernatural power of God to the city of East London, South Africa. Hundreds of people convened at one of the churches there. I'm sitting among the audience at one of the meetings where Penelope Quluba, a woman who had been diagnosed with colon cancer three years earlier was. Doctors had told her that the cancer was aggressive and could not be removed. They also said she would eventually become paralyzed and experience kidney failure. The only option was to put her on radiation and chemotherapy and that the cancer would take its course. In addition, Penelope had to undergo surgery to have a colostomy bag inserted. As a result, she felt self-conscious because not only was she sick; she also carried an unpleasant odor. After her diagnosis, Penelope regularly spoke healing over herself, declaring the word of God and telling her body that it was the temple of the Holy Spirit and had not been created with aggressive cancer or a colostomy bag. By the time of the meeting in east London, she was due to have more surgery because she had completed the chemotherapy, and the doctors needed to see what was happening in her colon. Apostle Maldonado gave an altar call for those who had cancer or HIV. Penelope made her way to the altar, where the apostle laid hands on her and declared her healed in the name of Jesus. Two weeks later, when she visited the hospital for the first time since the ministry event, the doctors were baffled when they found no trace of cancer! They removed the colostomy bag and put everything back to normal. Penelope is now free of cancer and full of vitality by the grace of God."[189] Guillermo Maldonado

Testimonial Two:

Healing of dropsy

"One little boy was healed of dropsy, stomach and bowel trouble. His clothes could not be buttoned because he was so badly swollen. The swelling went down at once; his mother fastened every button on his vest and clothes and stood him on the

---

[189] Maldonado, Guillermo. THE KINGDOM OF POWER: HOW TO DEMONSTRATE IT HERE AND NOW (SPIRIT-LED BIBLE STUDY). Whitaker House. 2013. Pg. 39

platform where everyone could see what God had done. The little fellow said in a clear, ringing voice that God had made him well."[190]

Testimonial Three:

Nervous Condition Healed

"Crafton, Pa. - Miss Hazel D. Benz, 20 Cleveland Avenue. I have suffered from nervous affection for five years. It arose from spinal trouble, the doctor said. I had no control over the muscles in my head. My face and mouth were constantly twitching and distorted. My eyes were similarly affected. I had moves about [sic]. Specialist after specialist was consulted. None of them were able to help me. They could not determine what caused the trouble. Finally, I heard of the meeting at the Sheraden Tabernacle. I came November 4th. When the invitation was given I went forward, was prayed for and anointed. The twitching and contortions stopped immediately and have not returned. In a letter written several months later, confirming her testimony, Miss Benz says: "Since I was healed of my serious nervous trouble four months ago, my mother, sister, brother-in-law and step-father have

---

[190] Woodworth-Etter, Maria. Signs and Wonders. Whitaker House. 1997. Pg. 83

been saved. I have myself gained eighteen and one-half pounds in weight."[191]

Testimonial Four:

Raising Of the Dead

"My friend said, 'She is dead.' He was scared. I have never seen a man so frightened in my life. 'What shall I do?' he asked. You may think that what I did was absurd, but I reached over onto the bed and pulled her out. I carried her across the room, stood her against the wall and held her up. I looked into her face and said, 'In the name of Jesus, I rebuke this death.' From the crown of her head to the soles of her feet her whole body began to tremble. 'In the name of Jesus, I command you to walk,' I said. I repeated, 'In the name of Jesus, in the name of Jesus, walk!' and she walked."[192]

Reports Of Divine Healing Conferences As Follows Via E Mail

Report Number One:

"Subject: Report on meetings--harvest time revival.
Date: Wed, 17 Jul 2013 09:45:20 -0400

---

[191] Bosworth, F.F. Christ The Healer. Fleming H. Revell. 1973. Pg. 218-219

[192] Taken from Apostle Of Faith by Stanley Howard Frodsham Copyright © 1948 by Gospel Publishing House. Pg. 58-59 used with permission from Gospel Publishing House. All Rights Reserved www.gospelpublishinghouse.com

Greetings in Jesus' Wonderful Name!!!--- what a time we had with Prophet Rohan this time around; where do I begin?-- First ,allow me to give God all the Glory-- and for sending Prophet Rohan our way!!-- What a blessing to have Prophet Rohan with us -- and of course I definitely can't forget Hamey!!----Hamey is such a blessing and a tremendous diamond in the rough---always shining no matter what!!-where do I begin? -- miracles upon miracles took place over these few precious meetings; souls saved; legs growing out-- (I can watch that a thousand times and still be excited as if it was my first time seeing it) ---this is what I have been preaching and believing for years-- I have experienced God's miracles over the years: but this time Prophet Rohan being used by God took it to another level!! PRAISE GOD!!-------the congregation will never be the same! Hallelujah!!-- oh yes-- gall bladder recreated; knees healed; joints and pain and arthritis; delivered and healed-- people coming out of walkers and walking again-- ears healed from deafness---on and on miracles after miracles-- what a time we had in God's Presence over the meetings--- God is and will be doing awesome miracles in the days and months to come---the congregation doubted at first (an honest doubt-- never seeing this before)-- but when they saw the miracles and healings-- it lifted their faith to an higher level in God!! ---- We are still praising God!!--- these are definitely the days of signs and wonders--- and just imagine that God used a Trini to work thru-- that's a miracle right there LOL--- Thank-you Prophet Rohan for obeying God in spite of set-backs and sacrificing -- you have -- have been-- and will always be a blessing--- stay sweet before the Lord as we continue to pray for you and the ministry.

Because of Calvary -- Pastor Wade and Grace and Harvest Time revival."

Report Number Two

"Subject: FW: SOM-Prophet Rohan-Report.doc Date: Fri, 18 Oct 2013 03:23:59 +0000

Shammah Outreach Ministries

Apostolic, Prophetic, Healing, Deliverance And Miracle Conference Report

Hosting: Prophet Rohan Rambally

October 12 and 13, 2013

Milton, Ontario, Canada

When one speaks of "impacting lives" you can rest assured that this is precisely what was taking place at the Shammah Outreach Ministries - Apostolic, Prophetic, Healing, Deliverance and Miracle Conference in Milton, Ontario, Canada where

Prophet Rohan Rambally was graciously hosted on October 12th and 13th, 2013.

As we girded up to receive the anointed man of God and the power of the Holy Spirit at the conference, Jehovah Elohim's stage was set and open to all believers and non-believers alike, as people from across the city and from afar were anxiously gathered and open to receive a divine touch from the finger of God. Whether it was a call to salvation, a prophetic word, a physical or spiritual healing, deliverance, or a miracle – the Holy Ghost was dispensing His supernatural wind of fire for the people of God and through God's precious Prophet.

Upon arrival, after traveling from Trinidad, we immediately entered into the throne of worship, praise and thanksgiving. This brought forth an army of ministering angels that joined to instigate the release of spiritual barriers and barricades and to move beyond into the presence and anointing of the Holy Ghost with the move of the apostolic, prophetic, healing and miracles with amazing signs and wonders! Miracles upon miracles, healings upon healings; souls saved, infirmities gone, sickness abolished, legs growing out, fingers realigned, hands brought back into alignment, a child's palette growing before our very eyes, another child's feet that were deformed brought back to alignment and the child walking normally again, unholy soul-ties severed, bold legs straightened to perfection, lumps in the throat dissolved, an arm that was paralyzed healed and now rejoicing in the Lord, heart disease crushed and healed, and ears healed from deafness, and so much more!!

We had prayed for this great move of the Spirit, been preaching it, teaching it, declaring it, proclaiming it and believing it for years, but this was definitely brought to an altitude that was beyond comprehension in the natural realm!! Yes, many came with a measure of doubt, but after all the exploits, signs and wonders demonstrated through Prophet Rohan – there was simply no question. The people experienced the power of our Father God first hand, and these signs and wonders that followed could not be denied. A new level of faith stirred up in the people and they were moved to heights that they never experienced before. The people experienced a tremendous encounter with Jehovah Jireh, our Provider, Jehovah Mephalte, our Deliverer, Jehovah Rapha, our Healer, and Jehovah Elohim, our Almighty God – yes, our Almighty God of second chances! What an awesome move of God, as the people worshipped, praised and rejoiced in their healing, deliverance, miracles and freedom! Praise the Lord.... Through this man of God lives were radically impacted for good through this powerful anointing and fire of the Holy Spirit ---

and, these life-changing victories in Christ are evidenced by the word of their testimonies. Hallelujah!!!!

What a glorious time we had in the presence of our Almighty Father, Son and Holy Ghost as He continues to do awesome and mighty things in the days to come! We give all honour and glory to God Who does it all and we thank Him for our precious Prophet Rohan whom He used mightily to bring forth the miraculous!! We bless Prophet Rohan unlimitedly, as he continues to pursue His divine presence and do the work of the Lord. For He is the same yesterday, today and forever and through His good and faithful, and most humble servant – we were truly blessed, healed and restored in Jesus' precious Name!

We thank our Abba Father, His precious Son, and the Holy Spirit for what the divine exchange on the cross and the blood of Jesus has done for us, and we give Him all the praise, honour and glory that He so vastly deserves --- for it is "Him" who does it all!

"And they overcame him by the blood of the Lamb, and by the word of their testimony; and they loved not their lives unto the death." (Revelation 12:11)

In Christ,

[213]

Todd Smith & Sandra Benaglia, Shammah Outreach Ministries."

Report number three:

"Visit Of Prophet Rohan Rambally To Nottingham, England On 14 And 15 February 2014

It was indeed a MEGA SHIFT and we praise God for what He did through his humble, committed and dedicated Prophet Rohan Rambally and his assistant Pastor Richard Alexander in England on 14 and 15 of February 2014! We are very grateful to everyone from the Prayer Command Centre for covering the conference in prayer.

The presence of God was very strong throughout the conference. And the atmospheric condition which was initially predicted by the Met Office to be stormy with heavy rain, had to submit to the authority and power of the Holy Spirit. We received testimonies of people being healed from all sorts of health conditions through the power of Jesus.

One lady was healed of cancer. She testified that she felt so much better after Prophet Rohan Rambally commanded healing in Jesus Name.

Several people were miraculously healed from arthritis, asthma, back and leg pains, shoulder and arm pains and other conditions by the ever present power of the Holy Spirit when healing was commanded in the Name of Jesus.

It was also a birthing chamber, where lots of delayed destinies and visions were birthed out as a lady contacted us about starting off her women's ministry, which she was never confident or courageous to start previously.

A lady with knee injury for 15 years, who had torn ligaments, and was scheduled for surgery after Prophet Rohan commanded the cells, tissues, ligaments to be healed in Jesus Name. She received her healing immediately. She was able to run, jump and dance in the presence of the Lord.

Prophet Rohan Rambally and Pastor Richard Alexander who were used mightily by God to pray strategically for the city of Nottingham, the surrounding area of the East Midlands in England. They brought the Word of God to us with conviction and power. They also spoke life-changing prophetic words in to the lives of many of the people, who attended the conference.

The powerful ministry of Prophet Rohan Rambally and Pastor Richard Alexander have had a major impact in changing the lives of people from all over England and from other countries in the world. The people, who attended the conference, not only came from Nottingham but also from as far as Leeds, London and Nigeria! We praise God for the signs, miracles and wonders, which we saw during the conference.

We are grateful to God for releasing his chosen vessel Prophet Rohan Rambally, in this season and time to our nation, England also Pastor Richard and the prayer warriors from the Prayer Command Centre in Trinidad and Tobago for their willingness to be used so powerfully by God. We have already received many testimonials of the which God has changed the lives of the people and awaits more testimonials.

May the name of the Lord be praised forever!

Amen.

Essence of life Empowerment,

Gloria & Christine."

Report Number Four:

"Report of Divine Healing Meetings with Prophet Rohan July 11 -12, 2014

Prophet Rohan and Brother Hamie came to Hamilton to minister prophetically and teach on Divine Healing.

Friday night started off with one lady being healed from a bad back and bad hip. The look on her face was incredible as she realized that she could now cross her legs where before it was impossible to do because of a bad hip. She could also now bend over which brought a look of astonishment to her face. We saw arches grow into people's feet that had flat feet for almost 20 years. Prophetic words were released and were very accurate.

We received this email from Lori

"I have a testimony to share. When prophet Rohan came to your home last month to do a healing school, I took the opportunity to receive healing for my finger. One morning in May, when making a smoothie for breakfast, one of my fingers had a run-in with my Cuisinart hand blender, cutting up mostly my fingernail, and a small bit of my finger. By the healing school I still had tenderness, nerve damage, and the beginning of a new fingernail.

When prophet Rohan ministered healing to my finger, he demonstrated to us how we can be a conduit of healing through releasing His Presence with a point of contact. He asked me to relax, and receive, so I closed my eyes and turned my heart toward the Father. Rohan held my finger in his hand, and continued to talk to the people in the room. I don't think he even addressed me, but the anointing fell on me as soon as he took my hand, and I could feel God's love and power flowing in. This was not ministering by 'commanding healing' as he had taught us earlier that day. He was teaching us something different. This was ministering by overflow. He was leaking God's Presence, and I was sopping it up!

That flow of love and power did some surgery on the nerves in my finger. The tingling was gone. It felt about 70% better. Glory to God! Rohan held my finger again…More love and power. Maybe he commanded healing - I don't know and I didn't care - I was just enjoying my Dad. Check finger - whoa. just a bit of numbness. 95% better. Hallelujah!"

I think the best part of the meetings was that the people, who were there, received the revelation of the teaching and then they went out and immediately started to heal the sick. Many of them stepped out the next day and started to command healing to take place."

Report Number Five:

"August 14, 15, 16 and 17 2014

Albany, New York

Berkshire Youth Center

Canaan, New York

Report of Meeting with Prophet Rohan Rambally and Brother Stanley from Trinidad

Meeting titled "Taking it Back to S.C.H.O.O.L. (Students Conquering Hindrances, Oppression and Opposition to Learning"

Praise the Lord from whom all blessings flow!!!! Upstate New York and the Berkshire Youth Center will never be the same after the glorious meeting we had this past week! What an amazing divine arrangement by our Almighty God Jesus

Christ the King. According to Rev. Kim Singletary --Chaplin at the Youth Center everyone is still talking about how blessed they were by the meeting.

All the glory belongs to God to align everything in the order in which he did. Who would have thought that the boys at the Berkshire Youth Center for troubled youth would not only be blessed by an amazing man of God but also by an incredible Teacher by trade!?!?! Surely we know that it was truly Christ in the making and planning of this event.

[219]

On Thursday when Prophet Rohan arrived and I picked him up from the airport the Lord told me he was pleased. Pleased that Prophet had accepted the invitation to come. Our initial prayer session in the Chapel with all of the leaders for the meeting Sis. Sandra, Rev. Kim Singeltary and myself along with Prophet and Brother Stanley confirmed that the Lord was pleased and that there was "a work that was dormant" and now being restored. Hallelujah Thank the Lord for being a God of restoration!!!.

On Friday night God did just that. Restored function to the limb of a young student of the Youth Center who was on crutches. It was absolutely amazing what I saw. Literally what I saw defied all the laws of Medicine. As a physician I literally had to rub my eyes to make sure what I was seeing was actually happening. Whoever says God does not perform miracles anymore should have seen what happened with this young man. As Prophet declared healing the boy's limb grew out becoming equal in length to the other leg all within a few seconds. He was able to walk away with the crutches in his hands holding them triumphantly in the air. Glory Hallelujah we serve a God who has given us power over sickness. I declare by His stripes we are healed!!!

Friday night was not only miracle night but was also a night where generational curses were broken. Things were truly shifted in the spiritual realm as Prophet Rohan prophesy to each young man who came. You could see how the Lord was dealing with each of them as declarations of health, success, prosperity and reaching their Divine destiny God planned for them was made. Amen!!!

Then there was Saturday night. For me it was like having desert after a delicious meal. What more could you ask for!?! The visiting local church "All Nations" were a blessing to the event. Having the choir sing and to see the Praise Dancers dance was such a delight. Prophet then used the spiritual uplifting from worship to catapult everyone to a higher level by displaying his God given gifts of teaching, prophecy and prayer. Through Divine Exhortation and Impartation Prophet distributed a Mantel to 4 people 3 women and 1 male. What was amazing was that the male identified was a Prophet as well and Prophet had never met him yet identified him. What a Revelation!!! Now to see a Prophet prophesy to another Prophet made me feel like I was reliving the Bible. Almost like when Elijah was prophesying to Elisha. Even the visiting Prophet said how blessed he was.

We serve an awesome God who knows how to take care of each[sic] everyone one of us...Leaders and all. Jesus Christ is truly our Father and our Shepherd.

Sunday concluded our meeting and just when we thought that since it was the last day of Prophet Rohan's stay that perhaps everything was over. Much to my surprise even when we were having dinner together before dropping Prophet to the hotel Prophet showed how he refuses to put our God in a box. Prophet Rohan even though we were in a restaurant amongst all types of people, showed how working in the prophetic is limitless. Why not!?! Don't we serve a God who is omnipotent? Glory Hallelujah!!! Prophet was praying and prophesying to all who would receive. It is truly God working through Prophet Rohan as he prophesized to my husband and he was completely on target with everything he said. We praise God for Prophet Rohan. He is a humble, loving steward of the Lord...Always displaying love and concern for those in need. What a blessing!!! We look forward to God sending him back to New York real soon. Amen!!!!

Humbly Submitted by a Sister in Christ."

Tanya D. Mays Jeune MD."

Chapter Sixteen

Conclusion

Healing is accessible to everyone, even in the twenty-first century. Healing should be a regular practice of each believer in Christ to manifest God's healing power. For many years different Christian denominations have disagreed about healing and its relevancy today. Is God's miraculous healing still at work today, or did it die out when the apostles died? The answer to this question is yes it is still available today!

Miraculous healing is achieved by precisely and accurately reproducing the instructions of Jesus Christ. This includes incorporating each of the three offices of God's government, the Priestly, the Prophetic and the Kingly into your ministry. These three offices are intertwined. First, you need to fulfill the obligations of the Priestly office: prayer, fasting, praise, worship and thanksgiving because this builds your relationship in God and produces faith of God.

An important factor in ministering to the sick is the need to forgive others, unforgiveness could hinder the flow of the power of God through you. Likewise believers should treat everyone they interact with as Jesus did. When you have the faith of God and the authority, sin cannot be a hindrance. You can now fully operate in the Kingly office and all commands that you give in the name of Jesus would be successfully executed. You are now in a position to receive the gifts of healing from the Holy Spirit and can administer healing in that avenue as well.

I have applied these principles to my ministry and have achieved numerous miraculous healings as presented in this manual. I am happy to say that God is still in the miracle working business and the death of the apostles did not change a thing!

Human beings suffer from sickness of the soul which is due to sin. Rom 3:23 "for all have sinned and fall short of the glory of God." Sin in our lives interferes with our relationship with God. Therefore God had a plan to deal with this human condition of sin. God sent His son, Jesus, to suffer, die and shed His blood on the cross for the sins of all mankind. When we confess our sins to God, acknowledge that Jesus rose from the dead, and receive Jesus into our hearts, we will be saved. Rom 10:9 "If you confess with your mouth, Jesus is Lord, and believe in your heart that God raised Him from the dead, you will be saved."

When we invite Jesus into our lives to be our Lord and Saviour, we become part of God's family, and we know we will be with Him in heaven after we die. If you have never received Jesus into your life, God is extending an invitation to you today to receive His love.

"For God so loved the world that He gave His one and only Son, that whoever believes in Him shall not perish but have eternal life." (John 3:16)

The following prayer is for those who desire to commit their life to Jesus Christ.

Simply pray these words sincerely from your heart.

Father, I come to you in the Name of Jesus. I accept Jesus Christ as my Lord and Saviour. Please forgive me of all of my sins. Wash and cleanse me in your blood. I believe that you died on the cross and rose again. I confess that Jesus Christ is my Lord and Saviour. Please teach me your Word, Holy Spirit, teach me to talk to you in prayer each day and guide me to a place of worship in Jesus Name. Amen.

BIBLIOGRAPHY:

1. Cerullo, Morris. The New Proof Producers. Morris Cerullo World Evangelism. 2008

2. Maldonado, Guillermo. Jesus heals your sickness today. ERJ Publications.2009. ISBN: 978-1-59272-337-9

3. Jenkins, Terrence. Nineteen Gifts of God to His Children. 48HrBooks. 1991. ISBN: 978-0-9784293-5-5.

4. Wigglesworth, Smith. Smith Wigglesworth on Healing. Whitaker House. 1999. ISBN: 0-88368-426-8.

5. Baxter, Mary K, Lowery, T. L. The Power of the Blood Healing for your spirit, soul and body. Whitaker House. 2005. ISBN: 978-0-88368-989-9.

6. Cerullo, Morris. The Miracle Book (How you can live in a rhythm of miracles using 5 simple steps). Morris Cerullo World Evangelism. 1984

7. Bosworth, F.F. Christ The Healer. Fleming H. Revell. 1973. ISBN: 0-8007-5124-8.

8. Liardon, Roberts. God's Generals - Why they succeeded and why some failed. Albury Publishing.1996. ISBN: 1888008-947-5.

9. Reid, John Howard. Prophet, Priest and King. Lulu.com. 2008 ISBN: 978-1435729902.

10. Eckhardt, John. Daily Declarations for Spiritual Warfare: Biblical Principles to Defeat the Devil. Charisma Media. 2011. ISBN: 9781616384432.

11. Wigram, George V. The Englishman's Greek Concordance of the New Testament. Hendrickson Publishers. 2006. ISBN 13: 978-1-56563-207-3.

12. Thayer, Joseph H. Thayer's Greek-English Lexicon of the New Testament. Hendrickson Publishers. 2007. ISBN 13: 978-1-56563-209-7.

13. Wigram, George V. The Englishman's Hebrew Concordance of the Old Testament. Hendrickson Publishers. 2006. ISBN 13: 978-1-56563-208-0.

14. Green Sr. Jay P. The Interlinear Bible Volume 1 Ed. Hendrickson Publishers. 1985. ISBN: 978-1-56563-977-5.

15. Hamon, Bill. Prophets and Personal Prophecy. Destiny Image Publications Inc.1987. ISBN:0-939868-03-4.

16. Chavda, Mahesh. The Hidden Power Healing Prayer. Destiny Image Publishers, Inc. 2001. ISBN: 0-7684-2303-1.

17. Blake, Curry. Divine Healing Technician Training Manual. www.jglm.org. 2006.

18. Lake, John G, Lindsay, Gordon. The John G. Lake Sermons on Dominion over Demons, Disease and Death. Christ for the Nations Inc. 1949. Printed 2003.

19. Woodwood-Etter, Maria. Signs, and Wonders. Whitaker House.1997. ISBN 13: 978-0-88368-299-9.

20. Cerullo, Morris. Victory Miracle Library. Morris Cerullo World Evangelism. 1986

21. McRae, William. Dynamics of Spiritual Gifts. Lamplighter Books. 1976. ISBN: 0-310-29091-0.

22. Cerullo, Morris. Lord Teach us to Pray. Morris Cerullo World Evangelism. 2004.

23. Maldonado, Guillermo.
The Kingdom of Power. Whitaker House. 2013.
ISBN: 978-1-60374-744-8.

24. Thomas, Charles R. Living in God's Kingdom on Earth. Xulon Press. 2007. ISBN 13: 978-1-60266-922-5.

25. Ekman, Ulf. The Prophetic Ministry. Word of Life Publications. ISBN: 1884017061.

26. Trimm, Cindy. Commanding Your Morning. Charisma House. 2007. ISBN: 978-1-59979-177-7.

27. Kirban, Salem. Discover Abundant Health and Happiness. Second Coming Inc. 2000.

28. Rubin, Jordan S. The Maker's Diet. Siloam. 2005. ISBN: 1-59185-714-7.

29. Maldonado, Guillermo. How to Receive and Minister Deliverance. ERJ Publications. 2010. ISBN: 978-1-59272-345-4.

30. Maldonado, Guillermo. How to Minister Deliverance. ERJ Publications. 2004. ISBN: 978-1-59272-151-1.

31. Maldonado, Guillermo. Prayer Discover the Secret to Effective Prayer. ERJ Publications. 2006. ISBN: 978-1-59272-349-2.

32. Maldonado, Guillermo. The Kingdom of Power Spirit-Led Bible Study How to Demonstrate It Here & Now. Whitaker House. 2013. ISBN: 978-1-60374-885-8.

33. Jenkins, Terrence. Free Indeed. Publish America. 2006. ISBN: 1-4241-5042-6.

34. Maldonado, Guillermo. How to walk in the Supernatural Power of God. Whitaker House. 2011. ISBN: 978-1-60374-278-8.

35. THE HOLY BIBLE. (King James Version) Brown and Marley.

36. Atkins, Robert. C. Atkins Diabetes Revolution. HarperCollins Publishers, 2004.

37. Cerullo, Morris. Demolishing Demonic Strongholds . Destiny Image Publishers INC.2012. ISBN : 9780768441932.

38. Agnes, Michael E. The Webster's Dictionary. Wiley Publishing 2003.

39. Hudson, Virginia Cary. Close your eyes when praying. New York: Harper & Row Hudson, 1968.

40. Tozer, A. W. The Root of the Righteous. Authentic Media. 2009. ISBN 9781850780687

41. Tozer, A. W. Man: The Dwelling Place of God. Authentic Media. 2009. ISBN 9781850780403

42. Hamon, Bill. The Eternal Church. Destiny Image Publishers Inc. 2003. ISBN 0768421764

43. Hamon, Bill. The Day Of The Saints. Destiny Image Publishers Inc. 2002. ISBN 0768421667

44. Green, Jay. P. Sr. The Interlinear Bible, Hebrew-Greek-English. Hendrickson Publishers. 2008. ISBN 9781565639775

45. Prince, Joseph. Destined To Reign. Harrison House. 2007. ISBN 9781606830093

46. Hamon, Bill. APOSTLES, PROPHETS AND THE COMING MOVES OF GOD. Destiny Image Publishers Inc. 1997. ISBN 0939868091

47. Trulin, Paul G. RESURRECTION LIFE. Harvesters Missionary Society. 1983. Moriah Publications Inc.

48. Trulin, Paul G. The New Testament Church in Today's World. Paul Trulin Ministries INC. 1987. Moriah Publications Inc.

49. Ridenour, Fritz. So What's The Difference. Regal Books. 2001. ISBN 9780830718986

50. Young, Robert. Young's Literal Translation. Robert Young. ISBN 9781781392324

51. Ibojie, Cynthia& Joe. Times of Refreshing, Vol two. Cross House Books. 2012. ISBN 9780956400888

52. Cerullo, Morris. Accepting Christ, Your Healer. Morris Cerullo World Evangelism. 2010.

53. Price, Charles S. Made Alive. Paul Trulin Ministries Inc. 1945. Moriah Publications Inc.

54. Damazio, Frank. Seasons Of Intercession. City Bible Publishing. 1998. ISBN 1886849110

55. Sandford, John, Paula. Healing The Wounded Spirit. Victory house INC. 1985. Pg. ISBN 0932081142

56. Reynolds, Joshua. 20/20 Brain Power. 20/20 Brain Power Partners LLC. 2005. ISBN 0976763303

57. Trulin, Paul G. <u>My Body His Life.</u> Paul Trulin Ministries. 1993. Moriah Publications Inc.

58. Frodsham, Stanley Howard. Wigglesworth, Smith. <u>Apostle Of Faith.</u> Gospel Publishing House. 1948.

59. Arayomi, Tomi. <u>Training Manual ESTHER PROJECT volume 3.</u> Tomi Arayomi February 6, 2011.

60. Resurrection Life / Dr. Paul G. Trulin. Moriah Publications Inc.

61. Made Alive / Dr. Charles S. Price co. Dr. Paul G. Trulin. Moriah Publications Inc.

REFERENCES / EXTERNAL LINKS

1. Devil put it back- The Refuge of Righteousness. <http://refugeofrighteousness.com/new/devil-put-it-back/> Retrieved on 3/31/14.

2. Cerullo, Morris. Prayer Manual. Morris Cerullo World Evangelism. 1996. Pg. 69-75

3. N.P., N.A. N.D. Definition of Authority. Dictionary.com. <http://dictionary.reference.com/browse/authority> Retrieved on 3/31/14.

4. WebMD. Leprosy Overview. WebMD. < http://www.webmd.com/skin-problems-and-treatments/guide/leprosy-symptoms-treatments-history> Retrieved on 3/31/14.

5. Yohannan, K.P. A Journey of Perseverance. Send! Vol. 33 No. 2. The John Roberts Company. July, 2013.

6. Timaru Bible Baptist Church. So you don't believe in divine healing either? <http://www.tbbc.co.nz/faq> Retrieved on 4/5/14.

7. Hamon, Bill. Manual For Ministering Spiritual Gifts. Christian International Ministries Network. 2004. Pg. 7, 8

8.   Rambally, Rohan. <u>Prophetic Miracles Part 1</u>.
www.youtube.com. 7/19/12
<http://www.youtube.com/watch?v=ZTFbIqH-pO0>